THIS BOOK BELONGS TO

_____

Joseph,

Thank you so much for your support

Steve

Publisher: **Anointed Hands Publishing Company**
P.O. Box 438741
Chicago, Illinois 60643
www.ninamotivates.info
anointedhandspublishing@gmail.com

ISBN: 9781513626079

DEDICATION

This book is dedicated to my children, Dezmarae and Kazual. I love you more than I can say or write and I hope this book helps you understand your father better. To my wife Tennille, thank you for keeping me upright and prayed up when the world didn't make much sense to me. Madison and Morgan, thank you for sharing your mom with me and allowing me to influence your lives a bit.

To my Father, You are the greatest man I know. Even to this day, I feel like that little boy who always needed you around. I love you dearly.

Mom, I would give anything to have Five minutes. R.I.P.

TABLE ON CONTENTS

CHAPTER ONE

NEVER HAD A CHANCE

It was a typical Saturday evening, and like always my dad was preparing himself for church tomorrow. My dad was always fly. As he laid his dark blue suit on the bed, I always knew I wanted to be like my dad. At the time I was eight years old, my father was my hero. He carried himself with a grace that I hadn't seen in another man. For what I knew, he was well-respected in the neighborhood and worked hard too. He was a deacon in our church and was always a father figure to my cousins and friends. Most importantly, the love between him and my mother seemed genuine and for a lifetime.

I remember one morning I was playing in the front room and my mother cooking in the kitchen. My father, fresh off a third shift work day came through the door. When my mother heard the door open, she came running out of the kitchen and leaped into my father's arms. I stood there watching my parents, and even at an early age, I knew that there was something special about what I was seeing. Without even knowing, my parents were an example of what love and a marriage looked like. My mother adored my father and my father adored her.

I grew up in a suburb outside of Chicago called Maywood. Maywood was a dope place that gives you a bit of everything. In the early eighties, white people still lived there, and everyone on my block treated each other like family. I can remember going to Fred Hampton pool in the summer time and making a little money shoveling the snow in the winter. I attended Garfield Elementary school, where I had an average education and teachers who meant well. I played basketball and Volleyball and had good grades. Life was indeed good for a young black boy.

I grew up with four other siblings. My oldest Sister Stacey was the rebel among us kids. My brother, Erick, was a shy kid who loved sports and keeps to himself mostly. My Other sister, Stephanie, was the apple of both my parent's eye. She was so sweet and compassionate and always doing the right thing. I had another brother named Jeffery, who at the time was in the army and my memories of him were vague. Then there was me, the youngest of them all who just tried to fit in anywhere.

We were very tight as kids. I recall a time when Stacey had a boyfriend at the house without permission. My mother and father gave clear directions that no one is to be in the house when they are not there. My mother would call the house on her break and want to talk to all of her children. She would ask us all the same question, starting with Stacey. "Is anyone in the house" and just like good soldiers, we all stated "no". Stacey, had her brothers and sister eating out the palm of her hand. She taught us at a young age that there will be no snitching and no matter what, we had to stick together even against our parents.

Soon after my mother called, she drove up into the driveway a few hours early. I was playing with a few friends a couple houses down, and I ran as fast as I could to the house to alert my sister. In all my years,

I never saw my mother move that fast. I assume she knew that the answers we gave on the phone was inaccurate and came home early to whoop ass. As I ran towards the house, I could see a person leaping out of the second-floor window where Stacey's room was. The person hit the ground, rolled a few times and leaped to his feet. I was able to make out who that person was; it was Darnell, Stacey's boyfriend and a common enemy to my parents. When I came to the door, I quickly realized I had made a mistake. My mother already had the belt in her hand and asking questions she already knew the answers too. "Since you little shits wanna lie together, you can get beat together." We all assumed formation, Stacey first, Erick, Stephanie, and lastly me.

We'd been used to getting beat like that, that it was almost comical. Stacey took her beaten like a soldier. Erick was my whooping hero, he would give the most awesome stare and once even grabbed the belt. Anyone who has ever taken a beating with a belt knows that it is almost a crime to grab the belt. When he grabbed it, the house went silent. I think my mother passed out briefly and then came too. Erick held on to that belt for what seemed like an eternity. My mom tried snatching the belt back, but my brother seemed to have the strength of ten men. With every second that he held on to that belt, his legend grew. I believe my mother knew that there was no chance of relinquishing that belt from my brother's grasp, so she started throwing closed fist punches, which by the grace of God she only had the energy for a few blows.

When it was Stephanie's turn, it was borderline pathetic. She would sob uncontrollably and plead for her life. I knew that her beating wouldn't be long and my fate was approaching soon. Everyone in the house knew my mother hated whooping Stephanie, so most times she would get a few lashes and her distress would be over. Two lashes in, Stephanie did the lowest of lows and began praying. It was the funniest thing I had ever seen, and I knew it had to be against all whooping rules and regulations. My mother had fallen for it and ordered her out of the room. My mother then focused her attention on me. Walking toward my position and the end of the bed, I needed a miracle. I thought this would be a good time for a telephone call to come through or a knock on the door, but no distraction would come.

Mom was loading up and sent a vicious lash across my legs. I really hated whooping, but I hated it more when my mom missed her designated target. I stepped back a little and went on to tell her that she hit me on the legs and I was sure my legs were broken. She looked at me and gave me that "boy please" look. I stepped back in for lashing number two and mom winded up and delivered the blow. This time I didn't run for cover and looked up and thought that was pretty weak. Mom had gotten tired, and that was primarily the case when she whooped us all. Out of breath, my mom told me to get the hell out of her sight and I better not lie again.

I went to the basement to meet with the other victims. After every whooping, we would meet to compare bruises and to make fun of each other. We would be there laughing and re-enacting each other's performance. Not one time did we ever blame the other for the mass ass whooping, we just tried to strategize on how to get away with it the next time. So many times we met in that basement, and we always promised to never snitch on each other and deal with the consequences if we got caught. Those basement meetings were one of many highlights of my childhood. The bond between brother and sister was powerful, and my parents knew they couldn't break that.

I never saw my parents argue or have disagreements. I assume if they did have issues, they did a good job of not sharing it with us kids. I had always thought we were rich or had a lot of money because when I went to the store with my mom, she always bought me a new action figure or all the fly suits my dad would had, But what really gave me that impression of wealth was when my mom bought my father a brand new Buick. That car had the whole block buzzing, and it looks terrific in our driveway. I remember other kids gazing at it in envy. It wasn't until then I realized that I was one of a few kids on the block that had both parents at home.

One of the kids, Mike, asked why my mother would buy my father such a nice car. I tried explaining that she just really loved my dad and she wanted him to have it. He went on to say that his parents were divorced and he only sees his dad on the weekends. I never heard that word divorce before, and never really gave thought to my parents ever being apart. For some reason, I was now intrigued about divorce and how Mike was handling everything. I must have asked Mike a million questions and wondered if I would one day be in the position he was in. Mike, explained in the beginning, his mom cried a lot and that his dad would buy him lots of toys when he came by on the weekends. He stated, that he really missed his dad being there and worried about his mom being alone.

I walked home that day feeling bad for Mike and the situation he was going through. I couldn't imagine my dad living somewhere else and only seeing him on the weekends. I wondered if my parent's marriage was as strong as it looked. I wanted to help my parents maintain their love for each other, but I didn't know how to do it. I wanted to sit them down and ask a million questions but was too afraid to do so. As I continued to walk home, I knew that I would never forget the conversation Mike and I had.

I guess that conversation with Mike wasn't by chance and definitely for a reason. I remember the day as if it was yesterday. It all started when my dad told all us kids to get dressed because we were going to the mall. He told us that we could have anything we wanted no matter how much it cost. Man, I was so geeked. I knew exactly what I was getting. When I got to the mall, I was going to patiently wait for my turn and head right to kids footlocker. The new "Air Jordan's" had just come out and I had to have them. I had seen a few kids at school with them and knew how expensive they were. I used to envision those shoes on my feet. I knew if I had a pair, I could play ball just like Jordan. We all walked into the footlocker, I was still hesitant to believe my dad would buy me these shoes. I assumed he didn't know the price and would give me a speech why they weren't worth the money. I walked along and spotted the shoes hanging gracefully on the wall. My heart started beating so fast, and all I was thinking was how fly I would be going to school Monday morning.

When the lady brought out my size, I was certain I was going to pass out. Man, those shoes fit like a charm and looked awesome on my feet. I looked up at my dad with the biggest grin on my face. He looked back at me and smiled. You already know, I wasn't taking those shoes off. I put my old shoes in the box and never saw those non-Jordan's again. As I walked out the store, I couldn't take my eyes off my feet. I had finally got a pair of Air Jordan's, and I felt ten feet tall.

When we pulled into the driveway, I jumped out the car and went strutting down the street. I had to show the world I was rocking Jordan's. I think I went to every house on the block telling them about my new shoes. I went by my friends Jesse's house, and he was shocked when he saw the wheels. We had always talked about what it would be like to have a pair, would we be able to dunk like Mike? So we did what all kids did when they got new Jordan's, we took it to the court. I was spectacular that day. I'm sure I had about thirty points and twenty rebounds in my new J's.

Later on that evening, my father gathered us kids and took us out to eat. Not really sure how we ended up at Denny's, but I was starting to get a weird feeling about everything that had happened that day. As I watched my dad fumble around the menu, I just knew this day was about to turn for the worst. After everyone had ordered, my dad gathered all of our attentions and starting tearing up. I was beginning to tear up as well because I have never seen this man, my hero, ever show so much emotion and pain. My dad reiterated that he loved us so much and that he and my mom were going to separate. As I looked around the table, there was a lot of shock and dismay. I recall Stephanie crying and Erick looking in disbelief. My father went on to say many other things in that restaurant, but I can honestly say I didn't hear a thing. I was sitting there thinking about the conversation with Mike and how all my fears had come to true. I wondered where my mom was and if she was ok. What was the reason behind the separation? Did he not love my mom anymore? Did she not love him? Whose decision was it to separate?

When we finally got home, I walked down to Jesse's house to tell him about what just happened. As I broke down the evening, my friend began to cry. I looked at him like "dude", I'm the one that should be crying. He explained to me that he too was going through issues with his parents and they would be separating soon as well. I was stunned. Jesse's parents seemed to have a loving relationship just like my parents did. Whenever I saw them together, they seemed so into each other. Jesse and I talked a lot that evening. We had no interest in video games or baseball cards, action figures or my new Jordan's. We talked about how our lives were going to change. We thought about being like Mike whose father was only around on the weekends. We both knew our childhood would never be the same.

A few days had gone by with no mention or action from my parents to separate. Had they made up, and now everything was fine? A few more weeks had passed by and nothing. Suddenly one Saturday morning, I was awakened to the sounds of my mother crying and the voice of my aunt in my parent's bedroom. I got out of bed to see what all the commotion was about and I saw what seemed to be my dad packing his things and my aunt trying to talk them out of it. I had never seen my mother cry so violently, she was pleading and begging for my dad to reconsider. I just stood there, off to the side crying until my mother spotted me and proceeded to close the door. This went on for what seemed hours, I went back to my room and prayed that my aunt could get my dad to change his mind, remind him how this would affect his children and that whatever was wrong, could be worked out. I heard my father's car start. He didn't even say goodbye.

My mother was never the same after that day, she seemed to fall into a depression that she could not pull herself out of. I didn't see my father again for about a month. There were no weekends at dad's place, he just drops by every once awhile and then he was gone again. We started to struggle financially, and the things that I didn't worry about were now a constant thought. Now, when I went to the store with my mother, I didn't ask for the toys like I used too. I knew money was tight and I didn't want to seem selfish.

I had a hard time coping with my father being gone. I missed those Saturday nights, watching him prepare for church the next morning. Not once did my mother talk with us collectively about how we were doing with the transition. That would have definitely eased the blow, but we never talked about our issues openly. I suffered mostly at school, I was disinterested and wondered what my father was doing and if he was ok. The only thing I could focus on was baseball and the team I played for after school. Every game, I would look out at the other parents and wonder if my dad was there, but he never was. I kept my feelings away from everyone except Jesse. He understood what I was going through, and we became each others therapist.

One day out of the blue, my father called and asked if I wanted to come to his house for the weekend. I suppose my mother had no idea what his intentions were because she frowned at the idea of me going. I really hoped my mom would let me go, I really needed to see where my dad lived. I wanted to make sure he was safe. But most importantly, I hoped he would talk to me about what was going on. As the weekend approached, I made a conscious effort not to ask my mom about my dad. I hoped he would just show up and take me with him without resistance from mom. To this day, I'm not sure why I was the only one going with my dad, I knew my brother and sisters missed him just as much as I did.

There was a window in my room that looked out onto 5th ave, just before Madison. I used to stare out this window often because there was always some action on 5th Ave. On that Saturday, I sat on the edge of my bed and looked out that window. Then, out of nowhere, I could see my father walking along that street. I was so excited to see him, it seemed like ages since the last time I saw him and wanted to be ready to go when he walked in. I ran down the steps to meet him at the front door and gave him a giant hug as I yelled "Dad." He was like a giant to me, I felt unbelievably confident and safe in his presence. He looked well, grew his beard out some more and was always fly. He asked where mom was and proceeded to go and see her.

Hour after hour had passed and my parents, whatever they were doing were still doing it. I waited downstairs playing with my He-Man action figures and saving the world from Skeletor. When my father emerged from my mother's bedroom, he came downstairs, and we prepared to leave. Before we left, I wanted to let my mom know I was leaving. When I got to her door, I could hear her crying, and she was lying on her bed. I wanted to run in and hug my mom, and I even thought of not going with my dad and stay and watch over her. I stood there for a second, puzzled about what to do. That day I didn't walk into that room and embrace my mom, I left with my dad.

I thought about mom the whole time I was with my dad, but I couldn't ignore how much I missed and needed this man around. My dad said he had a surprise for me that day and I was going to be very excited.

11

We caught the bus to Forest Park and got on the "L" train. I had never been on a train before but rode on the CTA bus with my dad during his work shift sometimes. After getting off one train, we boarded another going in a different direction. I had no clue where we were going, but it really didn't matter. When he stood up, I knew that was the sign that it was time to get off. When the doors opened, all I could see was Chicago Cubs signs everywhere. I tried to compose myself and not get too excited if I wasn't about to experience my first Cubs game.

My dad looked down at me and gave a small grin. Man, you have to be kidding me. Previously, the only time I saw the Cubs was on WGN, while my homie Harry Caray called the games. He gave the tickets to the attendant and I ran out to see the field. It was the greatest sight my young eyes had ever seen. We found our seats and I grabbed a hotdog while the Cubs battled the Cincinnati Reds. I recalled telling my dad that one day I would be playing ball in this very park and that he had to come to all my games. I didn't know my mom was keeping him up to speed on how well I was doing in the Little League, and he mentioned how proud he was of me. I enjoyed every minute being at that game with my dad. I fell even more in love with the Cubs that day.

After the game, we headed to where my dad lived. I had no idea what I wanted or needed to see. We approached a large apartment complex, which I learned years later was on the North Side of Chicago. When I walked in, it seemed small. I wandered around looking for things out of the ordinary. Why would my dad want to live here when we have a huge house with a lot more room, I thought. Nevertheless, I guess it would have to do for right now, I was just glad to be spending time with him. There were no televisions in the apartment that I recall, so entertainment would have to be generated by us. I don't remember what we talked about that day, but we talked a lot. My dad taught me how to make his famous cheesecake that the entire family loved, especially my cousins. Each ingredient has to be placed in separately, and the lemon juice is what's key, he explained. We ate cheesecake and was just father and son the rest of the evening.

I woke up the next morning excited about what the day would bring, but my excitement was brought to a halt when my father told me I could only stay one day instead of the whole weekend. My mom only gave me one day furlough, he explained. Just the day before, I had the most amazing time with my dad and wanted to stay another night and couldn't believe my mom would do this. As I packed my bag up, I tried intently to hold the tears that were brewing in my eyes. Whenever my dad asked me a question, I would answer him but never lifting my head up. I knew if I looked at him, I would burst out crying. When I gathered all my things, we headed out to take me back home.

As we walked towards the bus stop, I couldn't control my emotions and burst out crying. I grabbed my father's hand, and I stopped walking. Looking up at my dad, tears in my eyes, I told him I didn't want to leave and needed to be with him. I Imagine I caused a scene at the bus stop, but I couldn't help it. I didn't just cry for me, but my entire family. We all were hurting in different ways, and I just had to let my father know. My dad picked me up as he began to cry too. I was stunned when I felt the moisture on the side of his face. The man who was like a giant to me, my hero, my protector, cried with me. When he picked me up, we returned to his apartment. He put me down and went to his room and picked up the phone.

A few hours had gone by, and I felt confident that I would be staying with my dad for another night. I had made it up in my mind that I was going to ask him to come back home because we all needed him, especially me. I was going to tell him that mom seemed sad all the time and my cousins wanted cheesecake. As I sat on the floor in the living room of my father's apartment, I heard a loud knock at the door, I paid it no mind and continued playing with my action figures. Suddenly, my mom came into the room, and she had a look on her face that I had never seen before. She was visibly upset, hurt, and frustrated. Without being told, I went to get my bag from the bedroom. I wanted to cry again, but I knew that I couldn't. I didn't want my father nor my mother to see the tears and possibly cause more damage than I already caused.

When we got to the car, I was unable to control my tears and cried out intensely. My mother slammed the door and yelled at me for what seemed the whole ride home. I didn't mean to hurt her feelings, and I believed that was what I did. I imagined my mother thought that I was more loyal to the person who left us and not her. Things between my mother and I changed a lot that day.

CHAPTER 2

MINOR ADJUSTMENT

It's the summer of 1992, and my basketball card collection is the best in a five block radius. Upper Deck, had just come out with a USA Dream Team collection box and I had to have it. The complete set was very expensive, and I had no idea where I was going to get the money. One afternoon, I came up with the biggest idea a kid could come up with. The next, I will mark my place in history as the greatest card collector in Maywood when I go and steal the 1992 Dream Team Set. Why haven't I thought of this before? It will be simple, I thought. My mother was out of town, and my father is away at his apartment. I can just ride my bike, walk in, and make a quick getaway.

When tomorrow came, I sat out on my mission. The store was called Ventures, and it was located on Roosevelt road in Forest Park. When I made it to the store, I left my bike on the side of the building where the adjacent mall was located. I figured, I would walk in through the front door and exit into the mall area where more people would be, so I could blend in. I walk in, and there were a lot of people in the store. Perfect I thought. They kept the cards in a row, right alongside the register. I grabbed the box and looked at it for a second, trying to be cool and not tip the employees. Laying perfectly on the ground, was an empty shopping bag. I can just grab this bag, place the cards inside, and it would look like I bought it, I thought. Both items in hand, I walked towards the women's section which was right next to the mall entrance. I placed the cards in the bag and proceeded to walk out of the store. My heart was about to beat right out of my chest. I was about ten feet away from the door that lead right to my bike when I felt a hand on my shoulder.

BUSTED! The security guard grabbed the bag and had a tight, secure hold on my right hand. We walked back to the store and right into the back hallway. He made me sit down in a room that was littered with cameras overlooking the entire store. I must have counted twenty different small monitors that showed every square inch of the store. Sitting there, I thought of only one thing, my mother. I thought of many ways I could get out of this without her knowing. When security came back into the room, he sat down and started asking me a series of questions. Like a trained criminal, I said "I don't know" to every question he asked. He told me about the procedure when a minor was caught stealing from the store. I asked if he was going to call the police and if I was going to jail, he stated "NO," but needed to call my parents and needed my telephone number.

While my mother was out of town, my cousin Annette was watching us kids. When I gave the security officer my home phone number, I was praying my brother Erick would answer the phone. My brother and I were tight, and I knew he would help me get out of this jam without our mother finding out. When the security officer came back into the room, just like magic, he said your brother is on the way to sign you out. For a brief moment, I thought I was I in the clear when I

17

was reminded about the fine the officer spoke about earlier. He sat down next to me and gave me a form to fill out. The form needed my address, mother and father's name, and disclaimer at the bottom, agreeing to be banned from the store for one year. The total amount of the fine was $500.00.

When my brother got there, the security guard spoke with him for a few minutes, showing him the video of me trying to steal the basketball cards. When we walked out the store, I went to retrieve my bike, my brother burst out laughing at what I had gotten myself into. I asked him if he thought we could keep this from mom and he said "naw." Why not, I asked? You know mom comes to this store at least twice a week, and they are going to mail a letter home explaining what happened and a bill for the fine, he said. He thought I should tell mom about it right away and I thought that was the stupidest idea ever.

My mother came home a few days later, and I had no intentions of telling her what happened. Erick swore he wouldn't say anything although he took a risk harboring a criminal and not disclosing what he knew. Days turned into weeks and nothing from Ventures. I stalked the mailbox for weeks trying to intercept anything with that name on it. Just like my brother had said, my mom went to ventures twice a week and every time she came back, there was no mention of the great heist. A few more weeks had passed and still no letter in the mail from Ventures. I had completely forgotten about the ordeal until one day, I heard my mother scream my name while I was out in the back playing basketball. It was one of those calls that made the hair on my neck stand straight up. Before I entered the room, I thought of all the bad things I had done. My room was clean, I picked up all the trash in the yard, and I didn't hit my baseball and break any of our neighbor's windows, so what could it be?

When I entered the room, my mother was holding a letter in one hand and a belt in the other. "You stole what from ventures," she said. I proceeded to tell her about my day of the crime and hoping she would take pity on me. Pity, was not on the menu today as the belt came raining down on me. I tried putting on my best "you're killing me" routine, but she wasn't having it. As the beating continued, all I could think of was my dad. Maybe if he was here, none of this would have even happened. We would not have had money problems, and I just could have asked them to buy it for me like it used to be. When my mother hit me again, I stood there unfazed, and said: "I want my daddy." At that very moment, I knew I messed up. We both stood there in silence waiting for the other to make a move. My mother's face turns from anger to anguish, and she dropped the belt on the floor. She yelled at me to get out of her room, and we never spoke of the great Venture heist again.

As summer drew to a close and I prepared for the 5th grade, I saw less and less of my dad. Unlike previous years, my parents always got us new clothes and shoes to start the year. This year was quite different. There were no new clothes or shoes and very limited school supplies. My mother had done everything she could to keep us kids from going without, but I guess the absence of my father's income had finally taken it's

19

toll on her. I never knew what kind of financial arrangement my parents had, but I'm almost certain my father didn't pay 28% child support which is common today. During that school year, I took a lot of family problems with me. With my parental issues and financial issues, we had another bombshell to deal with when we found out my older sister Stacey was pregnant.

I was so uninterested in class, and most of my assignments were incomplete, and most days my homework wasn't finished. There was no one I could confide in about the issues I was facing. When parent teacher conference came around, my mother was either working or too tired to attend. When my report card's would come out, I would forge my mother's signature on it and return it without her seeing it. Many days, I would sit in class and day dream about quitting school and getting a job. I wasn't sure who would hire an 11-year-old kid, but I needed to help my mom and now help my sister. Most days I would go to school without eating breakfast because all we had was powdered milk and eggs that my mom would get from the church. I was never able to bring myself to eat the powdered version of real food, I was just to prideful. Things had gotten really hard for my family and I, and we never seemed to talk about any of it.

One day after school, I was walking home excited about the day I just had. Volleyball tryouts were tomorrow, and although there were never any 5th graders on the team, I was optimistic about my chances. That day, I walked with a kid named Levon, who stayed around the corner from where I stayed.

We didn't talk much, we just happened to be going in the same direction. When I turned the corner of 6th ave, I saw a man standing close to my house. I couldn't make out who the person was and chalked it up, as being anybody. As I got closer, the person started looking more and more familiar. When I got to the prairie path, I could see the man standing there was my dad. He had the biggest grin on his face, and I just took off, running to him. I was so glad to see him, it had been months since he came around. I remember jumping in his arms as we embraced each other. He went down to one knee and looked at me and said: "I'm home."

My dad and I went into the house, and he sat me down on the couch. He could see how happy I was to hear him utter those words. All the things I had been praying for had come true. My dad also told me he would never leave us again. I felt ten feet tall at that moment. Things were going to go back to the way it was when we were a family. When we had no money issues, no worrying about lights being turned off, no more seeing mom crying. I had no doubt that when my brother and sisters got home, they would be excited too. I felt the weight immediately leaving my shoulders. I could go back to being a kid, excelling in school, and quitting my make believe job.

Things seem normal for a few weeks, maybe even months, but you could see the strain that the separation had done to my parents. They didn't talk much around us kids, and we barely did things together as a family. I would come home from school and see my father downstairs trying to hide a beer from me, and my mother upstairs curled up in her bed. The most evident example that my parents were still suffering was the fact that my parents went to different churches. We had always gone to church together. Some Sunday mornings, my dad would take Stephanie and me to church with him early for bible study. On our way, we would stop at McDonald's and get a sausage biscuit which I loved dearly. But since my dad came back, my mother didn't want anything to do with our family church.

One Saturday afternoon, I went riding with my dad on his motorcycle. I remembered the routes well, and a few looked familiar. I knew we weren't going to Cubs game because the Cubs was in Milwaukee for a four game series. I wondered if we were going back to his old apartment. Did he leave something behind? When we got off the bike and proceeded up to the apartment, my dad pulled out keys and proceeded to unlock the door and walk in. When I walked behind him, the apartment still had the same furniture it had when I was there last. While my father walked into the bathroom, it gave me a chance to really investigate this place. I walked into the bedroom where the bed was nicely made. There were no pictures on the wall or the nightstand. Before I walked out of the room, something told me to look inside the closet. My parents had a real strict rule about going into other peoples closet, they hated it when us kids rummaged through their things. But I just had to open this closet. When I turned around to open the closet, I could hear my dad flush the toilet in the bathroom, so I quickly opened the closet door and was amazed at what I saw.

It wasn't long before my dad would pack all his belongings and leave again. This time there were no trips to the mall or family dinner to break the news. He had left again and didn't even say goodbye. Later on that evening, I overheard my mom on the telephone stating that my dad had gone back to another woman. She also stated that they met at the church we all used to go to. Immediately, everything started to make sense. That day at the apartment, I had seen women clothes in that closet and all along, my dad had left my mom for another woman.

I didn't know how I truly felt when my dad left again. I went to my room and hatched a devious plan. I figured if something traumatic happened, he would come back, and things would work themselves out. I decided I was going to get hit by a car. Sounds dumb, but I was desperate. Back in the day, my friends and I would play this game where we would run across the street nearly missing cars driving by. I'm not sure why we did it, but it gave me an incredible rush. So I gathered my nerves and went out to the front yard. About twenty cars rode by before I darted out in front of this passing car.

"BANG," their car popped me, sending me at least thirty feet in the air. I landed gracefully on the front grass of my house. I started yelling and screaming in fake agony. The car screeched to a stop, and the driver jumped out and ran towards the injured child in the grass. One of the neighbors ran and got my mom from the house. As I laid there, I believed that what I just did was the most awesome thing a kid has ever done. When I get to school on Monday, the other kids wouldn't believe it. They would want to sign my cast; where ever the cast would be? It would be awesome.

My mother came out, and I had a huge audience concerned about my well-being. Someone scooped me up and took me in the house. As I laid on the kitchen table, I knew I was near death. My father would have to come back and console the family, making everything right again. My mother looked at me, yanked my legs and arms back and forth and checked my head. When I opened my eyes, she was looking dead at me. "How did your dumb ass get hit by a car", she asked. "You're fine, go back outside but this time, go in the backyard, there are no cars out there", she said. No ambulance, no emergency room, and no cast. My plan was dead, all that for nothing.

CHAPTER THREE

SHE'S GONE

By this time, my mother had been going to Dialysis three times a week and had a Dialysis Catheter placed on her chest, just below her neck. She would get herself up and drive back and forth by herself. I never saw or heard her complain about what she was going through.

I now look back and realize that she was preparing to leave this earth. She would have intimate conversations that I didn't really understand at the time, but it seemed she had to say it anyway. One Saturday night, my mother and I were watching the color purple for the ten millionth time. When Mister, slapped Cicely for being out in the field reading and ignoring his calls to come and give him a shave. When Cicely, finished sharpening the razor and leaned Mister's head back and had to be stopped because she was going to cut his head clean off. My mother looked at me and said:" You know how not to make a woman want to kill you, right?" I looked up baffled and surprised and said: "I hope so." She laughed, but I could see her mind had gone to a very dark place.

Another time, I was in my room watching television, and she called me into her room and asked me to separate some clothes to be washed. I looked at her and thought, what the hell for. She started telling me how light clothes and dark clothes couldn't be washed together and how to read the care instructions inside the clothes. After that lesson, I had to grab the ironing board out of the closet, and she began to teach me how to iron a perfect crease. To this day, when I wash or iron my clothes, I think about my mother and do it exactly what she instructed me to do. Sometimes now, my wife gets upset with me because I won't let her wash my clothes. I had to explain to her that it wasn't just about washing clothes, it was about keeping a memory alive.

February 16, 1996, I had just turned 16, and just finished up drivers ED, and got my permit. I kept nagging my mom about taking me to the DMV to get my license, but every time, she would giggle and say "what car are you going to use?" "You're Van," I stated. "You ain't tearing up my van," she fired back. I told her a million times that I really was a good driver, and I promised not to tear her car up, but she wouldn't budge. Finally, I asked my homie, my big brother, if he would take me to the DMV and use his car. Like always, my brother came through and let me use his 1994 Chevy Corsica. My brother loved that car. He put some shiny rims on it and black tint that the police made him peel off a few months later. So the next day, my brother, I and the black Corsica went over to the DMV. On our way there, my brother was giving me tips on what to expect. He told me to make sure that I turn the radio off as soon as I put my seatbelt on. I said, "HELL NAW, I'm going to listen to that new Geto Boys." My brother looked at me and said: "shut yo dumb ass up and do what I told you!"

Man, when the instructor got in the car, the seatbelt was on, radio was off, and I was ready. He took me out, turn here, turn there, he instructed. After I did my parallel park thang, I passed. I was super geeked. I went back inside and got in line for the photo. I never smiled that hard in my life, I looked like I had twenty extra teeth in my mouth. When I walked out, I could see my brother sitting on the passenger side, he let me drive home.

It would be months before I drove again. Why was everyone hating on me? So when I got a call from this young lady asking if I wanted to go to the movies, I had to go. I had been trying to get with this girl for months, but she kept blowing me off because I was a sophomore and she was a senior. I could have had someone drop me off, but that would have been super lame. I needed to drive myself. So I went into my mother's room, and before I could even get it out, she said "NO." I went storming down to the basement and told my brother my dilemma. He pondered it for a while and finally said go ahead and have fun. Man oh man, my brother always came through. I got all dressed and headed out to the movie theatre in Hillside, and I waited and waited for this girl to show up, but she never did. I was pissed!!

My mother seemed to get weaker and weaker around the fall, 1996. So weak that one day she asked me to take the car and go get her something to eat. The irony, right? But I took the opportunity to establish trust with my mom and the car. I grabbed the keys, hopped in the car and drove two blocks to KFC. I ordered the food and headed home. Came back with the car intact and even had her change from the money from the chicken.

The next time I was given the opportunity to show off my driving skills was when my mom needed some medicine from the pharmacy on 13th and Roosevelt. When I got home from school, she was lying on the couch and complaining about a chest cold. When I walked in, she said, "take the car and go get my medicine from the pharmacy." I thought to myself, great, seven blocks this time.

For the next few days, my mother fought with that chest cold, and it seemed that it wasn't letting up anytime soon. The very next day, my mother's doctor had her admitted to Westlake Hospital, in Melrose Park. I don't recall, any of us being worried about the admittance. We took the opportunity to have the house to ourselves and have a little freedom. One day, two days, three days had gone by, and still, my mom was in the hospital, but this time they moved her to intensive care. My mother called me from the hospital, and she sounded like she never sounded before. I recall her asking me about school and saying that she was so proud of me. She asked me if I remembered all the things she had taught me and I said of course, I washed a load yesterday. I asked her how she was feeling and she said, "tired." I asked her when she was coming home and she said in a few days after some test come back. "Why are you so sick," I asked. She said that she thinks she has pneumonia, which I believed not to be a big deal. We talked for a few more minutes, and the last thing my mother ever said to me was "it's supposed to be cold tomorrow, bundle up."

November 8, 1996, was a gloomy and rainy morning. I remember waking up and looking out the window like "damn," I should stay home. I hated walking to school in the rain. I always felt like a wet dog the entire day. nevertheless, I got up, got dressed and headed out to school. As I walked to school, the wind blew ferociously and cut through my small leather jacket. I did not bundle up like my mother suggested the night before. As I continued, the wind seem to speak to me. As the trees, with its three different shades of brown whipped back and forth. I felt an emptiness that I never felt before and haven't felt since.

When I made it to school, I was indeed wet and smelled like a dog. Thankfully, I had gym third period, and I could take another shower and put on my Issey Miyake cologne. After gym, I headed to fourth-period lunch and sat in the back of the cafeteria trying to eat something. I had no appetite and really considered leaving after lunch and going home. I had Math next period, and I ditched that class at least three times a week. Before I left the cafeteria, I looked out the window, and the rain and wind were still at it, so I decided to stay and go to math.

I tried participating in class that day, but the emptiness I felt in my gut would not go away. All of a sudden there was a knock on the door and it was my cousin David, who was the Physical Education teacher and the varsity football coach. When he walked in, he whispered something at the teacher then set his eyes on me. He lifted his arm up and motioned me to come with him. David was a large man, and never smiled much when we were at school, But when I looked at his face, he had the most depressing look that I never saw on him. I quickly knew something was wrong.

When, I walked out of the classroom, my cousin said to come with him. I tried to figure out what he wanted as I ran down the many dumb things I was doing on a daily basis in school. We walked down to his office in the gym as he grabbed his jacket, still not mentioning why he snatched me out of class. Dave, "what's the deal", I asked. He finally stopped walking, turned to me and said that I had to get to the hospital as soon as possible. I keep asking him what was wrong, but he kept saying "we have to hurry."

I didn't even return to my locker to get my coat or books from my math class. We walked out the school, jumped in his car and headed to Westlake. We both were silent the entire ride there. I had so many things going on in my head. I knew I was about to see my mother for the last time if she hasn't died already.

When we got to the hospital and up to the ICU area, it seemed like my whole family was there. My aunt Annie Ruth, David's mother, walked over to me and smiled so wide at me. Darrick, she said, do you want to go in to see your mom? Is she dead, I asked? No, she is not, but she isn't breathing on her own. I told her that I would like to go in and talk to my mom.

When I walked in the door, there was another person in the room, but I could not make out her face. I took two more steps forward and turned to my right. When I turned right and looked up, I saw my mother sitting slightly up, her eyes were open and bloodshot entirely. She was not conscious and had tubes coming out her nose and mouth. When I saw that, my body quickly slammed up against the door, and I ran out, someone grabbed me and wrapped their arms around me and led me to the waiting room.

For a few hours, I sat in that waiting room numb to everything around me. As family members came in and out, I prepared myself for what already looked like my mother's death. There had been so many times that I watched my mom when she didn't know I was watching her. She would call out for my grandmother and say how much she misses her. Or times when she would break down and start crying for what seemed like no reason at all. Then there was my dad, who she never stopped loving and missed terribly. He was never coming back and she couldn't handle that. She was just tired.

After a few hours, I decided to go home. It was very quiet in the house, and I'm not sure where Stephanie and Erick were. I was where I should have been, a place where I spent numerous times before nagging, bugging, and even crying, I was in my mother's bed where I fell asleep. Across from my mother's bed was the biggest, ugliest alarm clock that still worked after all these years. As I was sleeping, there was a knock at the front door. My eyes shot open, and the first thing I saw was that ugly clock. The clock had 4:00am exactly in bright red across the front of it. There was no good reason for anyone to be at our door at this time, but to deliver bad news. I stood up on the bed and waited for whoever opened the door to start screaming. I heard the door open and brief pause, and

31

as expected, a scream. I laid down and went back to sleep.

For the next couple of days, the family did what every family does, preparing for a funeral, but I was trying to find an escape. The more people that came by the house asking me how I was doing, the more aggravated I got. I wanted to kick it with my brother, but he mostly stayed in his room, he and Stephanie were devastated. We all were, but I knew my devastation was for a lifetime, so I decided not grieve all at once.

I was keeping it together until I decided to go to my mom's room and chill, I figured I would be alone in there. When I opened the door, my father was there sitting on the radiator where I saw him sit so many times before. Whenever he came by after leaving, he would sit on that radiator across from my mother's bed, and they would talk for hours. Now, he was in that same familiar spot. But this time, it was different. My dad sat there with tears engulfed in his eyes. I kneeled down at the foot of the bed across from him. We didn't speak, we didn't need to. Our tears said it all.

CHAPTER FOUR

A BROTHER'S LOVE

During the funeral, I watched from afar how my mother's death affected my brother. Before the funeral started, he was in the waiting area of the church, and he could not stop crying. I was so hurt for him, my sister's, and the rest of my family. I saw my mother's death differently than everyone else, and I mostly worried about what would become of us kids. Would my father come back to get me since I was the only one left that was a minor, or would I go live with him?

I'm not sure when my brother and I became best friends, but I knew he felt an obligation to me when dad left. Whenever he bought something for himself, he bought the same thing for me. When he was wrestling in high school, he would take me to practice with him and make sure I learned the moves also. We shared the same void left by our father, but as kids we never discussed it much. My brother wasn't and still isn't the one to express how he feels about something. He mostly would shrug it off as if he didn't care. Nevertheless, he was as gracious as a person could be during those difficult times with dad leaving and mom dying.

Right before mom had died, I started paying more attention to the ladies and experimenting in sex. My brother knew I was a virgin, but also knew I was trying to change that as soon as possible. By the time freshman year had come along, I was determined to start having sex. It seemed like everyone in High school was doing it except me. I had a steady girlfriend and was trying daily to get some of her. Jokingly, my brother would tease about the fact that I hadn't scored yet. But little did he know my time was approaching soon. My girlfriend Jana, told me the night before that she didn't want to go to school the next day and would be asking her mother if she could stay home. She told me if she did stay home, would I be willing to ditch school and spend the day at her house. I thought that was a pretty dumb question because I ditched school at least once a week anyway for no good reason.

So when morning came, all I had to do was wait for Jana's call to see if she indeed was staying home. I was hoping like hell she was, because I had to get this monkey off my back. A few minutes went by, and Jana called and said she was indeed staying home. I hung that phone up so fast, ran down to the basement to my brother's room, searching high and low for a condom. Today had to be the day Jana gave me what we called in that day the "Monkey." I took a condom from my brother's stash, ran out the house and around the corner to throw my mom off just in case she was looking out the window. Jana lived about three miles away in Broadview. I ran like I never ran before. What normally was an hour walk took me 30 minutes, I was hyped. When I got to the corner of 21st and Roosevelt Road, I had to wait on the side of the local bank because her mother's car was still in the driveway. The anticipation was killing me, and finally, Jana's mother pulled out the driveway and headed off to work. When she turned the corner, my sprint continued.

When she answered the door, she had her pajamas on and a blanket over her shoulders. She had played that "I'm sick" role to a tee. She let me in, and I went downstairs. We had the entire day to ourselves. Her older sister wouldn't be getting home until after 3:30 and her mother an hour after that. No matter what, I had to be out of this house at 2:30 and make it back to my house around 3:45 to not have my mother suspect anything. For the first few hours, we just sat there on the couch and watched television. During that time, Jerry Springer was huge, and we watched episode after episode. Around 1:30, I started getting nervous that I wasn't about to enter manhood and have sex for the first time. I had to make a move. So, I said to Jana, "That was the last episode of Jerry Springer, what should we do now"? She said those magical words, that every teenage boy wants to hear from a girl. "Whatever you wanna do," she said. Eyes big, and trying hard not to look desperate, I went in for the kill.

For years, I was sneaking and watching Cinemax late at night, and I figured I would just do what I saw on television. We started kissing and I started moving my hand down to where her pajama bottoms were, and started pulling them down. Now, if this wasn't going to happen she would have moved my hand away and told me to stop. But man oh man, she let me continue. After both of us were bare assed, I went into the bathroom to put on the condom I stole from my brother. I had no clue how to put that thing on, so I

35

pondered for a second and thought about not putting it on at all. I stared at that wrapper intensely looking for some sort of directions, but they must have forgot to put it on there. Jana then yelled out "you good", and I yelled back, "yea." I didn't know if it was on inside out or upside down but it was on nonetheless. I opened the door, walked out and gave away my innocence.

We laid there for a while, not knowing what it was we just got done doing. I couldn't believe that I had finally did it, but was a little confused about what all the fuss was about. Jana and I, had been going together for a while and truly believed we loved each other. We never considered the risk or even talked about them. I assume the only reason why she did it was because of the enormous amount of pressure I put on her. I had been hinting about sex for at least a year before that day. I assumed Jana, was a virgin too, but I never asked. The whole time we kept asking each other if the other was ok. We had ascended into grown folks territory, and there was no turning back.

Around 2:30, it was time for me to head home so I can arrive at the designated time. I was on cloud nine and couldn't wait to tell my brother what just happened. As I walked, I started having mixed emotions about what I just did. I was thinking how my father would react to what I did. I had so many questions about sex, and I wanted to talk about it with him. Whenever my father spoke, I hung on to his every word. I always wanted to impress him with my grades and sports accomplishments. I'm sure if I had the sex talk with my dad, he would surely tell me to wait until I got married and that's what I would have tried to do. He never knew the impression he had on me and still probably doesn't. Nevertheless, in his absence, there was my big brother Erick.

So I came running down 6th Ave, with the world's greatest news to share. I see my brother in front of the house talking with our neighbor. I come running up to him with this quirky grin on my face, and I just stare at him. He looks back and quickly said, "What did you just do?" "You know," I said. He looked me up and down for a second and said: "No, you didn't!" "Yes, I did." My brother's face quickly turned into anger. Come in the house, let me talk to you, he said. We went into the kitchen, and he asked me to tell him the details, and I did. The whole time I was telling the story, his angry face didn't change and he shook his head momentarily in disapproval. After I had told him the details, my brother went on to tell me how stupid and disappointed he was.

My brother went on to explain that I had made a terrible mistake and I should not have gone to that woman's house and had sex. At the time of my scolding, I'm kind of looking at my brother sideways because he's the one who let me listen to Eazy-E and 2 Live Crew. He went on to say that he wanted me to concentrate on my school work and especially sports. My brother had always been my biggest fan and believed I could be really good at baseball and basketball, if I stayed with it. What if she gets pregnant, he said. Do you have money for pampers and milk? What if you catch a disease? All these things my brother was trying to drill in my head, were things

I had not thought of. He walks out of the kitchen and back outside. I sat there really confused but knew what he was saying was right. He was always trying to teach me something, and I always tried to listen.

CHAPTER FIVE

BOY MEETS WORLD

Months after my mother's death, everyone was still adjusting to life without her. My father was at the house every day, and for a while I believed he was moving back. After a few weeks, he returned to his life, and I started mine. I wasn't too upset when he went back to his home, I was too concerned about what I was going to do with myself. In a matter of months, I went from structured family home, to making my own decisions and coming and going as I pleased.

When I went back to school, I had no clear direction of what I was doing. It was really hard to concentrate on academics when you're worried about your next meal or if the light were on when you got back home. I started spending most of my time ditching class and looking for girls.

One day, my dad came by to talk to my brother, sister, and I about some money that was left to us by our mother; around twelve thousand for each of us. My dad asked us all that we wanted to do with the money we received, and there was no question what I wanted to do with mine. I wanted a car and not just any car, I wanted a 1985 Cutlass Supreme. Man, that car was so dope to me. There were a few dudes around town who had that car and every time I saw them, I hated a little bit. So, when I told my dad what I wanted to do with my money, he agreed with the decision. I searched high and low, through every car magazine and couldn't find this car.

I started to forget about the car until one afternoon, I was in the car with my brother, and we passed a car lot that had the cutlass stuck in the back with a for sale sign on it. When I noticed it, I almost passed out with excitement. I yelled at my brother to make a U-turn and go back. When we entered the lot, there she was a 1985 gray Oldsmobile Cutlass Supreme. I grabbed my Primeco cell phone and called my dad. I asked him if he could come up there right now and bring some money.

The dealership wanted four thousand for the car but would need some engine repairs. My dad and I took it for a test drive, and I fell in love. When we got back to the dealership, my dad and the manager talked details while I stayed next to the car smiling from ear to ear. When my dad walked out, I noticed he had the keys in his hand. The car was mine.

When I got the car home, I could not believe I had the car that I always wanted. I stared at it for at least an hour before I decided to go show it off. When I jumped in the driver's seat, I realized I needed some banging music, so I went around the corner to the local radio store to grab a tape. When I got there, I already knew what I was going to get. The Notorious B.I.G. Hypnotize has just come out, and that song was a banger. I grabbed a copy, threw the money on the counter and skipped out the door. When I got back to the car, I put the tape in, turned the volume up and pulled out into the street.

I can't really explain the feeling, but I was on cloud nine. I drove around Maywood at least fifty times, blasting that same song until I was almost out of gas. When I finally went home, I stared out the window at my car for most of the night, and couldn't wait to drive that car to school the next morning.

While my social life was definitely on track, my grades were still terrible. So terrible that Junior year, I was held back. Things around me started to crumble. I'm not sure what it was exactly that got my mind back on track, but I started to take my academics seriously again. One morning, I decided to go see my advisor and ask her what I needed to do to get my missing credits, so I could graduate with my original class, class of 1998. She told me if I took a few classes at the local junior college, I could earn the credits I was missing.

So, I decided to take a few courses at Triton community college. Lucky for me, it convenient and easy. I would go every Wednesday night from 5-9pm for 8-10 weeks. After I passed the class, they would send transcripts back to Proviso East. One Wednesday night, I sparked up a conversation with one of my classmates named Victoria, who was taking a course for job reasons. Victoria was twenty years older than me, but we were both from Maywood and her daughter, whom I knew went to school with me. We talk much in the class about the course work and her family. She told me about her husband and children then asked me if I knew her daughter, but I told her "no." Not sure why I told her I didn't, but I lied nonetheless. After class, we went our separate ways,

41

and I thought nothing of the conversation with Victoria.

Early that Saturday morning, my brother and I were outside in the front yard lifting weights. I'm not sure why we were in the front yard, but it probably was the most ghetto thing my neighbors had ever seen. That particular day, we were working on chest and back and had the bench set up with the bar and about 145 pounds on it. Also, laid to the side were dumbbells, to do bent over rows. Whenever we would work out, my brother would have the radio on, and we just would go through a routine non-stop for about an hour. I must have been in a zone because I didn't notice Victoria was across the street at her friend's house. I had no idea she was friends with my neighbor, so I waved to them both and continued working out.

When I went to class that following Wednesday, Victoria sat next to me. I went through the class like always, reading the chapters assigned and doing the class work. When class was drawing to an end, Victoria reached back and handed me a note. The note simply stated if I would be interested in going to get something to eat after class. I wrote back, cool and that I would meet her in the parking lot after class.

After class was over, I went outside and hopped in the car with Victoria. We drove off and started chatting about the class that was almost over. Where do you want to go? she asked. As a true sixteen-year-old, I blurted out McDonald's as she giggled and nodded in agreement. So we drove and talked, and I noticed we just passed our third McDonalds. I started thinking is she about to kidnap me or something, but I looked her down and thought she couldn't if she tried. Victoria was petite and short, with a beautiful black skin and short hair.

As she made a left, we entered into Hillside movie theatre and went straight to the back where it was dark and isolated from the rest of the parking lot. She put the car in park and cut the engine off. I was still confused about why we were here and hoped she didn't forget about the McDonalds as my stomach growled. She looked over at me, and the conversation got sexual. She asked me first how good I was at keeping secrets and I assured her that I don't gossip at all. Before I could get those words completely out, she started kissing me.

Before long, she had placed her hand on my leg and was trying to locate my zipper. The whole time I was thinking that this can't be happening and that she was married. As easy as it was to think that I also was thinking don't be a punk, show her what you can do. Before you know it, we ended up in the back seat of her car.

The entire ride back home, I was totally tripping. On the one hand, I felt like a grown ass man, and secondly, I felt bad for whoever her husband was. When we got close to my house, she dropped me off in the alley so her friend would not see us together. When I entered the house, my brother looked me up and down, gave a little stare but didn't say anything.

He always knew when I was up to no good, but this time he didn't lecture me.

I really needed to talk to my father. I thought about calling him but didn't know exactly what I should say. I had much more encounters with Victoria, but the one that stands out and really made me think about what I was doing. One time, she took me to a local motel and taught me how to please her. The entire time she gave me step by step instructions on how to do it, where to touch, and many other sexual requests. After she was done, she took me to McDonald's and gave me twenty dollars.

That night as I laid in my bed, it started to dawn on me that this older woman was molesting me, but I was confused because I was enjoying it and getting money and food. I started to ignore Victoria every time she would page me, and I guess she got the picture that I wasn't interested any longer but her impression lasted quite a while with me. After my ordeal with Victoria, I had a hard time being interested in girls my own age and spent the next few months engaging woman who were a few years older, mainly college girls.

I never mentioned to anyone what I had gone through with Victoria. Months later, I told Erick and he thought I was nuts. I never told my dad even to this day. I knew he would have been furious if he found out when it was going on and maybe would have yelled at me. That would have been great to have my father yell at me. I was always looking for his guidance on things like that. My time with Victoria would have never happened if my dad had been around.

Months later, I was outside my house, and a car pulled up. I recognized the car, it was Victoria's, and she pulled into my neighbor's driveway. When the car opened, a man stepped out and went up to my neighbor's house. This dude was the biggest human being I had ever seen, easily 6'7 330 pounds. It was Victoria's husband, and he looked pissed. When no one answered after ringing the bell, Bigfoot looked directly at me and motioned me over. I know I died numerous times as I walked closer to this dude. He asked if I seen my neighbor that day and told me when and if I did to call him. Apparently, he and Victoria got into a huge fight and she was missing. I just nodded my head and got far away from him.

Junior year of High school was going to be dedicated to academic achievements and floating under the radar. My eventful summer was enough excitement for a lifetime, and things at home weren't the best. So, when I bumped into Kim, I was dealing with and facing a lot. She was walking in the hallway and I like always was shooting my shot and flirting a little. Before I knew it, I had walked her all the way to her locker and forgetting that I needed to get to my own class. We exchanged numbers that day and decided to keep in touch.

Kim and I hit it off immediately, and it was odd because we knew each other since freshman year and even had a few classes together, but never looked at each other in that way. Kim's family was very nice and warm in the beginning. They treated me like a part of the family, and I guessed they knew the difficulties I was facing at home. Erick, Stephanie and

45

I were the only ones living in the house. My father went back to the residence where he and his Girlfriend lived. We barely had food in the house, and everyone was just trying to survive. Some days, I would go to school and haven't had a meal in days. But at that time if you saw me in school, you would think everything in my life was great. I never complained or told anyone what I was going through. I was even able to maintain and keep some focus in class.

I don't think Kim or her family will ever know how much I appreciated everything they did for me. One afternoon, things came to a head at the house between Erick and me. I had worn a shirt of his without asking, and we started to argue. My brother never before cared that I wore his things, as long as I didn't destroy them. At the time my brother was struggling to find a decent job and going through some things with his lady. When he asked about his shirt, we began to argue, and I mentioned something about him just being mad because he had woman problems. Erick picked me up so fast and slammed me on the corner of the bed. As he was hemming me up, I threw what must have been a soft punch, because it didn't phase him one bit. After the blow had landed, he reached back with a punch of his own, which landed square on the side of my face. After he hit me, he let me go, and I knew he regretted it, and he walked out of the room. I got up and went to the bathroom to access the damage. The left side of my face looked like I was hit by a truck. I immediately started to cry. Cry, not because he hit me but because the struggle that we were going through had become too much for us all. Never in a million years would my brother punch his little brother, whom he treated like a son. The pressures was to much.

I called Kim after that and explained to her what happened. She told me to come over to her house where I stayed for a few days until things blew over with my brother. Things got worse after the fight with. Early one morning, I was running late for school. I quickly got dressed, grabbed my car keys and headed out the door. When I made it to school, I parked in the student parking lot and headed to class. When I bought my car, my father had a kill switch installed in it. My kill switch on my car was right below my steering column. When the switch was enabled, the car would not start, making it hard to steal. So, when I got out my car that morning, I forgot to click the switch.

When seven period was over, I went my locker, grabbed the books I needed to study with and headed towards the student parking lot. When I got to the lot, my car was gone. I searched around for broken glass, but there was none. I hoped I was being pranked, but that thought quickly left. I looked all around trying to remain cool as other students were getting in their cars and driving off. I started walking towards Kim's house a few blocks away. As I walked down Washington, the only thing I thought about was my mom. I had taken this money she left me and bought this car, and now the car is gone. Why didn't I use the money for something better, something that she would have approved.

When I reached Kim's house, I told her and her family what happened. They called the Maywood Police Department, and I filled out a report. I then called my dad and told him the story. He told me that he would see me tomorrow and that he would handle everything else. Kim dropped me off at home, and I went to sleep, which I did a lot during that time in my life.

The very next day, I was walking down Ninth Ave towards Roosevelt road with a couple of my friends. It had to be around seven or eight because it was getting dark. When we passed this one house, this guy walked off the porch and began walking behind us. We continued to walk not paying the guy much attention, but as our walk continued, he got closer and closer, and then we started paying more attention to him. We decided to slow down and let him pass us because we felt something wasn't right. We figured if he wanted to fight, he was outnumbered. It couldn't be a gang thing because we all lived in the area and were not gang members.

Just when he was about to pass us, he turned around and pulled out a gun. As if it was yesterday, I remember him saying "everyone gets in the gang way." We all scattered and started running. When I took off, I slipped, and that totally changed the direction I wanted to go in. My intentions were to run up ninth avenue, but when I slipped, it turned me completely around, and I was running into someone's back yard. When I looked over my shoulder, this dude was running behind me. When I slipped, my shoe came off, and I had very little traction. As I ran to the back yard, the world's tallest fence awaited me. I didn't know where to go, and he caught up to me. He raised the gun to the back of my head and told me to give him all of it. My leather coat, my gold chain, and gold bracelet. It felt like a lifetime trying to take all those things off. When I handed him the things, I never looked back at him. When I gave him the last item, it was a long pause that seemed like an eternity. I was certain that he was going to shoot me, but he just stood there with the gun to my head. Finally, he ran off, and I took the biggest deep breath I had ever taken. I was in complete shock and don't know how I made it to the 7/11 on ninth and Roosevelt.

I sat in the store for a few minutes and tried gathering myself. I had no idea where my friends had went and decided to just walk home. So shocked from what just happened, I walked past the very house that the guy came out from. When I got home, my dad was there, and when he saw me, he knew something was wrong. I had mud all over my pants, and I looked like I just saw a ghost. When he asked me what happened, before I could get a word out, I just broke down. Everything I was going through, my mother's death, my car being stolen, my fight with my brother, being robbed at gun point, just came pouring out of me. I quickly told my dad the story and just wanted to be done with it. I didn't even want to call the police to make a report. I was tired of talking to the police about people taking things from me. I just wanted to go in my room and of course, sleep.

I spent most of the summer with Kim. I stopped hanging around my friends who I learned weeks after the robbery, that they were indeed involved with gangs. That summer also was a very violent one around Maywood. A lot of friends who I went to Elementary school with, were killed or facing long prison sentences. I didn't want any part of getting in trouble. Before school let out for the summer, a friend talked me into selling weed with him. My drug dealing only lasted one day because my stash fell out my pocket in Biology, just seconds after my teacher was helping me with a question. I gave my homie the money I owed and flushed the weed down the toilet. It wasn't for me.

Also that summer, I started hinting around to Kim about us finally taking that next step and have sex. She wasn't having it and quickly shot those ambitions down. Kim was a really good girl. Did well in academics, was a part of the Proviso East dance team, and by all accounts a virgin. She had a wild streak that afforded me to grab some booty from time to time, but she made it clear that she wanted to wait until marriage to have sex. On the surface, I made it clear that I was ok with that, but in my mind, I had other plans in mind.

As the Senior school year started, Kim and I became one of those couples around the school and had an air tight relationship. I got off to a slow start academically and was close to falling back into the trap that had me a year behind my graduating class. One morning, I decided to stay at home and not go to school. Around 9am, I got a call from Kim that changed the way I felt about her and my future. She told me that she was very disappointed that I wasn't in school, and I had an hour to get to there, or the relationship was over. I can't be with a loser she said, you are too smart to be acting so dumb.

Her level of love and concern was something I had been searching for, for a long time since my dad left and my mother died. Her concern was genuine, and I fell completely in love with it. I got out of bed and got to school before the third period had started. I never ditched school again, and from that point on, I was completely dedicated to graduating. Everything between Kim and I wasn't glorious. We had more differences than we had in common. So much difference that I knew deep down that we wouldn't last. I was in a dark phase in my life, and I held on to anything that gave some sort of happiness.

As time went on, Kim and I became closer and closer and the only thing missing was we had not been intimate yet. I was hinting around it almost daily, and she would give me the same answer every time, but I was breaking her down slowly and slowly. So after a few more months, I had given up trying and didn't mention it at all. One day Kim called me over and told me to hurry up. When I got there, she was home alone, and she took me to her bedroom. We talked for a while, and we started making out, and she allowed me to touch her in places that were recently off limits. When she let me pull her shorts down, I couldn't believe what was happening. The relationship went to the next level.

I'm not sure why she decided she was ready, I had let up on the pressure. All summer long we explored each other and falling deeper in love with each other. The loneliness and isolation were only growing at home, and I spent most of the time away. There was no certainty there. I thought one day I would come home and there would be a lock on the door, it made coping and relaxing there almost impossible. The only thing I had was my siblings and Kim.

As our senior year was coming to an end, Kim and I started preparing for prom. She had come up with this crazy shade of orange, and I decided to rent a cream tuxedo. When I went to get fitted for the tuxedo, Kim rode with me and was very quiet the whole ride there. When we pulled up to the shop, she blurted out a very serious question. "How would you feel about having a baby right now?" She asked. Not really feeling that, I answered. Her demeanor quickly changed, and she had a look of defeat in her eyes. I just stared at her for a moment, and she tried intensely not to make eye contact. I must have called her name at least six times before she raised her head up with tears in her eyes. Darrick, I'm pregnant, she whispered. I fell back into my seat, a million things just popped into my head. I immediately felt guilty. Kim had so much future ahead of her and knew exactly what she wanted to do and having a child at eighteen wasn't one of them. Furthermore, her family had no idea she was even sexually active and wouldn't believe it if you tried telling them.

We sat there in the car for hours talking about what we were going to do. We never talked about her getting an abortion, not even once. Kim's entire fear was telling her family and their reaction or and disappointment. My fear was of a different sort. I worried about how I was going to support a child. I told Kim that we had to get her to a doctor to make sure she was ok and find out how far along she was. Kim was under the assumption that we could simply go to her doctor without her guardian finding out.

We argued for days about telling her family, but she wasn't having it. One evening, we were at her house and had the appointment with her doctor the following day. I told her that when we show up for the appointment that they are going to call someone before they see you. I told her that I had no choice but to tell someone because her health was at stake. When I got up to go upstairs, she fought me like a dog, but I managed to break away from her and went upstairs to her aunts' room.

When I reached the room, her aunt invited me in, and I sat down. For some reason, I wasn't afraid or nervous at all. I had been through so much up until then, all I wanted was help and guidance. I looked her auntie right in the eyes and said: "Kim is pregnant." The room went silent for what seemed an hour. She looked at me and told me to go down and have Kim come upstairs and then asked me to leave. I did as she asked, gave Kim the message and I left. On my way home, I thought about how I was going to tell my father. I was hoping like crazy it would bring us closer together and maybe he would guide me through this whole process. I gave him a call and asked if it was possible for us to get together.

The following day, Kim and I went to her doctor's appointment and just as I told her, they wanted to call a guardian. We both were relieved that everyone who needed to know, knew. Everything went well at the appointment and we prepared ourselves to be parents. To say things between her family and I changed would be an understatement. Before the pregnancy, they treated me like family and let me participate in family functions. They even used to let me spend the night at the house. But when Kim got pregnant, all that changed and I expected it. The thought of me sexing their niece and granddaughter was probably too much to bare, so now I had a certain time that I needed to leave, and I never spent the night again.

My dad came by the house early that Saturday morning and asked if I still needed to talk to him. I got out of the bed at met him downstairs in the kitchen. We had small talk for a minute, and I just came out with it. He'd met Kim several times and seemed to like her very much. What I wanted most was for my father to go crazy, to start screaming at the top of his lungs, but he didn't. He asked if I loved her and I stated "yes." That was it. That was the only question my father ever asked his 18-year-old son, soon to be father. To say I was disappointed would be correct. Why couldn't this man, give me more than he was giving?

Prom came and went, and graduation was quickly approaching. I had done very well for myself. I was on the Honor Roll and started to be fond of Psychology and Sociology. As the date got closer and closer, I was getting more nervous about my future and the baby arriving. I had no intentions of going to college and didn't remember anyone ever asking me if I was. I planned to get a job and take it from there. I had no direction and was simply satisfied with graduating on time. Graduation day was awesome, we had our ceremony outside, and Kim's family had a party for her and invited me and my family.

The day after graduation was a somber one for me. Just like that, I went from a student with adults who cared, to a young man with twenty dollars to his name and a baby on the way. I put my clothes on and went to the local store to grab a newspaper to rummage through the classified section. I had no idea what I was looking for and just jotted a few numbers to call, once I got home. Customer Service, fork lift driver, security guard, is all I could possibly qualify for. So I gave these jobs a call and fortunately, I scored some interviews. I ironed my best-pleated pants and found a brown flowery tie. I was so used to wearing Jordan's and Pelle Pelle coats, that this new attire was foreign to me. (Victoria, bought most of the designer clothes and shoes I owned)

Interview after interview, I heard the same things, not enough experience. I grew tired of searching for a job and felt defeated. Kim was getting bigger, and the pregnancy was moving along. I stayed away from their house most of that summer because I felt embarrassed about having no future and no job. I was determined not to give up and go out into the streets and do what my friends were doing. Then one day my luck changed, I got a call from this company called

55

Navistar. They were an airport parking company that transported people to Ohare Airport. I went on the interview and was hired on the spot.

Basically, all I needed to do was park the customer's car, hand them a ticket and carry their luggage to the shuttle bus. I made $7.50 an hour plus tips, and my coworkers were cool to work with. A job like that is cool in the summer time, but when winter time came around, I couldn't maintain and I quit. I DID that with no new job or a backup plan. I wouldn't find another job for many months later.

As I stated earlier, I tried my hardest to avoid being around Kim's family, but when it was time for her baby shower, I had no other choice. When I got there, I was one of two men that were there, and there had to be about fifty women. I tried my best to stay out the way and help out when I could. When it was time for her to open all the gifts, they asked me to sit next to her which was hard to do, when you have so much self-loathing going on. There had to be at least a thousand gifts, and most of them came from her brother. This dude loved his sister and spoiled her as much as he could. Whenever she opened a gift from him, it was the most expensive shit ever. He brought about 20 boxes of pampers, clothes, shoes, diaper dispenser, stroller, every damn thing you could imagine. I never felt so small and useless in my life. I know he wasn't purposely trying to embarrass me, but I could not help and feel that way. I promise you, we didn't buy pampers or anything until the baby was about 7 months old.

In early January, 1999, the due date for Kim and I had come and gone. We spoke to the doctor, and he wanted to induce her on the 9th. So I went over to Kim's house to help her pack and be of any kind of support I could. While I was in her room, I overheard a conversation her aunts were having about me. They were saying how I was never going to amount to anything. How I didn't even have a job to buy Pampers. They both laughed, and the bashing continued as I tried not to hear. I looked over at Kim, and she heard what was being said too. She could see how hurt I was. I looked at Kim and asked her to say something to them, but she didn't. I wanted her to take up for me and not act like she didn't hear what was being said. I really needed her to defend me, tell them I was trying, I needed her support. Kim didn't say a word.

I grabbed my shoes, as tears of anger balled up inside me. I told Kim I would pick her up in the morning and I walked out the house. On my way out, I had to pass the very people who talked about me like a dog. I never raised my head up, and I didn't speak on my way out. By the time I reached my car, I was sobbing uncontrollably. To this day, I can't truly express how I felt at that moment. It's something that I've never forgotten and what still drives me to this day. When I finally made it home, I opened the front door, and all the lights were out. I tried flicking the switch in the kitchen, but nothing happened. Our lights had been turned off a few hours earlier, and I just lost it. I grabbed a baseball bat that was lying near the back door and began swinging it violently in the kitchen. I bust the glass stove, dented the countertops, and put numerous holes in the wall.

I felt like I was going to throw up, so I ran upstairs to the bathroom and dropped to my knees. I had my head completely submerged into the toilet and still crying uncontrollably. I remember calling out for my mother and asking God to help me. Then out of nowhere, there was a hand on my shoulder. When I looked up, it was my big brother. He could see that I was struggling and figured that I had reached my point. He never asked me what was wrong or what happened, but simply said, "whatever you are going through, you will beat it. You are a very special person, and mom would be proud of you." Erick, my brother, my friend, saved my life that night.

CHAPTER SIX

DEZ

The next day, I was going to be a father. I was 18 years old and did not have a job. I managed to get myself together to graduate from high school, but hardly had a place to live. My mother was dead, and my father was in and out. The only thing I knew was that I was going to be the best father I could, but I didn't know what that looked like or how to do it. I was at my lowest point and had no confidence at all. Kim had an amazing support system that should have made me feel better, but it only made me feel worse. The things I couldn't do, they could and would probably make me feel bad about doing it. I thought long and hard the night about running away, never to be heard from again. I always wondered if my father thought of me during that stretch in my life. I wish he could have been there for me.

January 9, 1999, started off terribly. There was a major storm that dumped a large amount of snow in the area. Roads were closed, and if you didn't have to be out, you didn't go out. I had to get my pregnant girlfriend to the hospital to deliver a baby. I got up and put on two layers of clothes and went outside to dig myself a path out of the driveway. Three hours later, I'm still battling the snow. By the time I finished, I had an hour to get dressed and get Kim to Westlake hospital. When I picked Kim up, she came wobbling out of the house and got in the car. As we set out to begin the first stage of rest of our lives.

We entered the room, and the nursing staff got everything prepared to bring in the new life. I sat over in the corner looking clueless and paranoid. Minutes turned into hours and still no baby. Suddenly, the contractions began to come more frequently with more pain. The nurse came in to see how far dilated she was and announced that it was time. She walked out to get the doctor, and when he returned, it was time to push.

As the pushing started, Kim's mom and I were scared to death. We stood behind Kim's head holding hands. The doctor, sounding like a play-by-play analyst, was giving every detail. "The head is out" he shouted. At that very moment, I thought I was going to pass out. I made a mistake and looked down there and saw only a head, and got woozy. Kim pushed a few more times, and Dezmarae Infiniti Campbell, came into the world. At first glance, I thought this was a very weird looking kid. Her body was covered in blood, and other things I didn't recognize and her head was stretched out like a cone. Just when I thought it was over, the nurse handed me a pair of scissors and asked if I wanted to cut the umbilical cord. I quickly gave her the scissors back and declined that request.

Mom and Baby were good, and we were all moved into a different room. When Dez was brought in, and I got to hold her, the feeling was all too surreal. As she laid there in my arms, I thought about how I would do anything for her. I also began to feel sad about all the people who were absent on that day. My mom, who would have just adored Dez and those big legs she had. My father, who I wish could have been there just for moral support. After all those thoughts had settled, I began to think about how was I going to support a child and a girlfriend. It was a grueling problem and I had no solution too.

A few days after Dez was born, a friend asked if I could drop him off downtown, to take a test for the Illinois Department of Corrections. I agreed to take him and only asked for a few dollars for gas. What he didn't tell me that the test would take at least an hour to complete. So instead of sitting in the car and waiting, I decided to give it a shot and take the test as well. The test was broken into three parts, written, physical, and an Interview. I sat down for the written test and could not believe how simple it was. They put on a video, and when the video was complete, answer questions about what you just saw, basic comprehension.

The physical section of the test was a test of strength and endurance. First, I had to complete twenty push-ups and twenty sit-ups. Secondly, I had to run an obstacle course that had to be finished within one minute. Third, there was a two-minute endurance test where I had to step up and down on a box. Lastly, there was a short interview that I was most concerned by. I remember sitting down at the table, and I was holding one of Dez's pampers. When the interviewer asked me about the pampers, I told him that, I am doing this for my daughter and her mom. They went through a few more questions, which I believed I answered correctly. Before I left, they took fingerprints, and if everything checked out, I should receive a call.

Months had gone by and no call from the State. That was a difficult few months, trying to find a job and not contributing to Dez's well-being. After I heard what Kim's aunts were saying, I spent less and less time at their house when they were there. When I did come around, I felt like the spotlight was on me. I was hesitant to change a diaper or feed Dez, remembering the words that hurt me so bad before. It seemed like every time I was around the subject of me having a job came up, or what was Kim and I going to do next.

Once again, I was at a point where I didn't know what I would do next. Job interviews came and went without any calls offering a job. I started avoiding Kim and Dez, staying away for days at a time, because I was too ashamed to show my face. Again, I thought about just running away. Like always, Erick would always throw me a few dollars and make sure I had something to eat. Every once in a while, he would make me take a drive with him, and we would see a movie, or buy something for Dez and make me tell Kim it was from me.

One afternoon, my luck started to change. I was sitting in my room, and my cell phone rang. When I answered it, the voice on the other end was a woman from IYC- St. Charles, and wanted to know if I was still interested in working for the state of Illinois. Trying to compose myself, I stated that indeed, I was still interested. She gave me instructions to come by the institution to take a drug test, and if everything clears, you start the job May 10, 1999. When the conversation ended, I fell to the floor, thanking God for His mercy and grace. I was so excited and so relieved. I called everyone to share the good news.

The next day, I went out to the Institution and took the drug test. There were ten other applicants there as well, and everyone looked excited to get going. Soon, I realized that I was the youngest applicant there. I was two months removed from my nineteenth birthday, but that wasn't going to stop me, I was going to nail this opportunity. We all sat down in the conference room and was given a description of what was to come next. Although we all were just hired, there was one more step to take before you were certified. Each of us had to go down to Springfield, for a six-week para military training. We would stay on campus five days a week and come home on the weekends. While in training, I would be earning a salary and health benefits would start immediately. Every Monday morning, a bus will leave from Statesville Correctional Center and take us and all the new trainees from around the northern district to Springfield.

May 10th, had come and the day before I spent with Dez and Kim. I woke up so early because I was having problems sleeping and I didn't want to over sleep. I threw my bag in the trunk and drove about forty minutes south to Crest Hill, where Statesville is located. The Institution had a parking lot where trainees could park our cars all week. I took a spot on the bus, and we headed out on the two and half hour drive south to Springfield. As we drove, I started thinking about all the things I wanted to buy for Dez when I got my first check. I also decided that it was time for me to move out of Maywood and get my own apartment.

When we pulled up to the training academy, it seemed deserted. All of sudden about six men dressed in army fatigue ran on the bus and started yelling and cursing, telling us to get off the bus right now and line up outside. It was so unexpected. Some people started arguing and cursing back at the men. I was still in a state of shock when a guy jumped in my face yelling something about my major malfunction. Before I opened my mouth and put my foot there, I remember being told that the training was paramilitary. Instead of talking, I grabbed my things and exited the bus, falling in formation like I was told.

Other trainees were having difficulties following directions, and many arguments were going on around me. Each trainee that talked back was asked to go back to the bus, they were just fired on the spot. I checked my emotions and pride real quick. I really didn't care how much they yelled and cursed at me. I wasn't going to mess up this opportunity. I needed that salary, and I definitely needed that health insurance for Dez. After the dust had settled, they separated the men from the women and walked us to our dorms. I also noticed that we were separated from the trainees going to the adult division. Each of us was given a number after attendance was called. I had the number one (1) which meant I was on the first floor of the dorm and each room will hold four trainees.

When I got to my room, I met the three other trainees that I will be spending the next six weeks with. Alba, was going to IYC-Chicago, Steward, was going to IYC-Joliet, and Johnson, Joliet as well. We had ten minutes to get settled in, and be outside for further instructions. Once outside, we were given a tour of grounds and gave very strict rules. There were no cell phones allowed, but there was one pay phone in the lobby to share with everyone else. Lights out were at 9pm, and I had a little alarm clock radio that didn't pick up any urban channels. The only channel that came in clear was a country pop channel.

Early the next morning, the floor leader kicked in the door yelling and screaming about being outside in five minutes with shorts and gym shoes. When I looked over at the alarm clock, it read 5:00am. When I got up, got dressed, and made my bed (bed making was a real big thing, really big), I went outside. All at once, everyone started falling out the door, wiping their eyes, wondering where the fire was. The squad leader yelled out "its jogging time."

Again, there was nothing they could say or do to make me not do as I was told. I had a purpose bigger than their insults or morning jogs. I was determined to get through these six weeks and take care of my daughter. After we jogged, we went back in to get ready for class, which lasted until 4pm. During class, we were introduced to policy and procedures and went over incidents and how to report them accurately. The class time was very helpful in understanding what it was I was getting into. I was preparing to go and work in a prison, a place where I could easily be injured or killed.

After the first week was over, we boarded the bus and returned to Statesville. I drove home and spent the weekend telling everyone who would listen about my first week, ESPECIALLY KIM'S FAMILY. I was always so eager for Monday to come so I could get back to Springfield. For some strange reason, I thought of training as my going away to college. I knew with a new baby and a new job, there was no way I would ever have the opportunity to go away to college. So for six weeks, I turned the training academy into the University of North Carolina.

It was a sad day when I successfully passed everything at the academy and was graduating. A lot of those people I grew fond of, and knew I would never see again. The day of the graduation, Kim surprised me and drove out and had baby Dez with her. When we marched in, I could hear Dez saying "da da" from the bleachers. It was a very proud moment for me, I felt accomplished, but the highlight of the evening was when I was handed a full check and my health insurance card. The next time Dez went for her checkup, she will be using Blue Cross Blue Shield.

The State of Illinois, had deemed me qualified to be a Correctional Officer, and I was ready to start my career. That Monday after graduating, I reported to the 6am-2pm shift and given keys to a housing unit and was told to shadow for the entire week. That first day was nuts. There were three different fights, and I had to get into the middle of it. After every incident, my coworker and I, would talk about what happened and write a detail report. When you are walking into a setting like that and being the new trainee, you get tested a lot. My first day, week, and month was nothing but a big test.

I also had something else working against me, and that was my age. Some of the youth I was supervising were either older or the same age. I had made a choice, just like all other personal information, to keep my age a secret from youth and most staff. What I had more than any other officer was relatable insight on how the youth may or may not be thinking. For the first few months, they would size me up, and I did the same to them. When they talked tough, I talked tougher. When they challenged me to a fight, I would always accept. Fortunately, it never came to that. As time went on they understood me and how I did things, and I understood and respected them.

There was something else that was helping me be a great officer. I had never been around so many educated, experienced, and well-traveled black men. I would just sit and listen to them exchange stories of sacrifice and triumphs. I got some of the best relationship advice ever just listening to some of the things they had been through. They motivated me to think bigger and to always carry myself with integrity and character. Back in the academy, I dreamed of going to college, and one day I did, but the education I receive from these men was priceless. I wanted to learn how to do the job the way they did, so I continued to listen and I study them.

So when the money started coming, I decided it was time for me to get my own place. I talked to my brother and sister, and they also were making plans to leave the house we grew up in. When my search started, I knew I wanted to get closer to the institution and also be close to Dez and Kim. I went to the Walgreens and grabbed one of those apartment finders books, I scanned through and saw a nice apartment in my price range. I called the number and made an appointment to go see it. I don't recall Kim and I ever talking about moving in with each other at that point. So when I went to see the apartment, a one-bed room was what I was looking for.

The apartment was southwest of Maywood, in the suburb of Westmont. It was just what I needed at the time, not too big and not too small. It had a pool that was directly outside of my patio, and a laundry room nearby. I had mixed feelings about having my own place. I had no idea how to live on my own, how to pay bills, and budget my finances, but I was determined just like the new job of not failing. It was really time to grow up. I went to a local bank and opened an account, and had payroll at the job set me up with direct deposit. I had all my bills come directly out of my account on a certain day, and I took a course on money management online. I was growing up, making sound decisions, and learning how to be a man.

I was enjoying my independence, but I knew it wouldn't be long until the conversation came up about Kim and Dez moving in with me. I avoided the conversation as long as I could, but one day Kim's mom brought it up. I wanted to be honest and tell her I needed more time to figure this whole thing out, but that's not what came out of my mouth. Instead of telling the truth, I stated that Whenever Kim was ready, she could just move right in.

After a few weeks had passed, I had totally changed my view on living with Kim. I was seeing Dez, and her every day and it felt good taking care of them. We would alternate nights cooking, but that usually ended up ordering out. Kim decided to take a break from some college courses at The Illinois Institute of Art, to find a job. Kim always spoke about one day being a fashion designer, and I knew one day she would return to school to make that dream come true. When she found a job, I took her to the Oldsmobile Dealership and bought her a car right off the showroom floor. It was a white, 2000 Intrigue. Things were looking up, but issues were right around the corner.

When I got closer to my lease renewing, Kim started hinting at possibly getting a bigger place. That may have well been true, but what she was really saying was, she wanted a place that was both ours, not just mine. I understood how she felt and agreed to find something bigger, but it had to be closer to my job in St. Charles. She agreed, and I told her that she could look for a place and whatever she liked I was cool with. A few days later, she came back and said she found a great 2 bedroom apartment in Naperville, right off the expressway. When she took me to go see it, I instantly liked it. The apartment sat on a golf course, and the rent was reasonable. We signed a lease, paid the deposit, and moved in a few weeks later.

It wasn't long after we moved in, that the issues started. Let's just say, coworkers of the opposite sex on both our parts were putting a strain on the relationship. I'm sure nothing ever came of any of it, but trust had been broken, and it led to a lot of bad decisions, arguments, and name calling. The atmosphere had become so toxic and the belief that the other was untrue that I decided to move out. I was so done with the relationship, I signed another lease at a different apartment complex in West Chicago. I was on the verge of buying new furniture and having the utilities set up.

As much as I loved Kim, I knew deep down we should have parted ways then. Whatever we said to each other worked, because I did not move out. We took a bandage and placed it all over the issues we were having. Never told an adult what we were going through and never sought professional help. We were basically two twenty-year-olds trying to figure this family thing out. Looking back, that year was the beginning of the end for us, but both of us were to scared to face that reality. We both wanted Dez to have us both around and was willing to sacrifice for that, but we were not honest with ourselves.

CHAPTER 7

KAZUAL

Kazual Jalee Campbell, was born June 16th, 2002. When Kim was ready to go into labor, I learned from my previous mistakes and went downstairs and made a lunch, packed a bag, and grabbed some magazines. As I packed the bag, Kim began to yell that there was no time and that her water had already broken. So I began to pick up the pace. I was able to get her downstairs and into the car. I drove around the corner to pick up her mom and began speeding down Eola road in Naperville. We got settled in the room, and I went to my familiar place in the corner and began reading a magazine. As Doctors and nurses came in and out the room, I maintained my distance from Kim because she became very agitated and I didn't want no problems.

I felt a little bit more confident this time around. I had a great job with benefits, two new cars, and our own home in a great neighborhood. Although Kim and I were still not married, I didn't have the anxiety and nightmares that hindered me when Dez was born. A few hours after we got to the hospital, Kim was ready to start pushing. After a few, my son came into the world. When I got my first glimpse of him, we all noticed that he had grey eyes. After doing a triple take and cursing uncontrollably in my head, I turned to Kim and gave her a look. She looked back at me and said: "Boy, please, don't even go there."

Just like Dez, he was beautiful. Straight black hair and those Grey eyes, which the doctor assured me would change. We all stayed overnight, and the next morning we all went home. I was able to stay home with both mother and child for two weeks, thanks to the Maternity leave at the job. During that time, I held that boy all day every day. I was trying to avoid losing that precious time as I had done with Dez. So when he went to sleep, he did it on my chest. When he was hungry, I prepared bottles and fed him.

Quickly after Kazual was born, Kim fell ill again. Unlike with Dez, the episode lasted longer and was extremely aggressive. We started to correlate these aggressive episodes with child birth and started having talks about permanent birth control. I recall Erick mentioning that he had had a vasectomy a few months back and the procedure went well. So Kim and I researched Vasectomies and if this was really something we wanted to do. We discuss everything from our ages to the fact that we weren't married. We both agreed that we were content with having just two kids. We had our girl and boy, and they were only three years apart. I was all in for the vasectomy. When I called my insurance provider, and they said the procedure is covered 100 percent. The only thing left to do was make an appointment. Also, I didn't want Kim to endure any more pain. We had also discussed her getting her tubes tied, but didn't want her to risk any more complications, so I needed to do this for her.

I was twenty-two years old, and I was about to make a permanent life decision. Besides my brother, there was no other man around to advise me on what to do. I did not reach out to my father and tell him about what I was thinking. I assured myself that he would not give me the advice I so desperately needed, so I tried asking guys around the job what they thought about the procedure. Everyone I asked, had some testosterone filled answer on why they would never get their nuts cut on. When it was all said and done, I had to protect Kim, so I scheduled the appointment.

On the day of the procedure, Kim was ready and excited to get going. In all my years knowing her, she was never ready or on time for anything. When we got to the clinic, they ask again was I sure I wanted to do this. I assured them that I was and I wanted to go on with it. I was ushered into a preparation room and was asked to take off all my clothes and lay on the table. The anesthesiologist, came in and asked me to count to ten. Before I could get to nine, I was out. When I woke up, the procedure was complete. I tried walking, but the effects of the anesthesia left me unable to function on my own. I do recall, Kim driving home and trying to get me up the stairs, but struggled badly. When I finally came to the next day, I was still lying on the stairs with an ice pack between my legs. Apparently, I was too heavy for Kim to get me up all the stairs, so she left me there to sleep.

After the vasectomy, Kim and I were sitting on the couch one evening, and the topic of marriage came up. She asked me what were we waiting for and I told her nothing. We starting talking about a date and before you know it, we were engaged. There was no ring, no dropping to one knee, no blessing from the parents. Just two people with two kids, living together agreeing to spend the rest of their lives together. I truly loved Kim, but we had our many issues and we were trying diligently to work through them. Kim had a way of making me feel like she was the more superior parent. She would often times undermine a decision I made concerning the kids which would always turn into a huge fight. I wanted to make an honest woman of her, I knew having two kids and not being married was a huge burden for her.

With all that playing in my head, the real reason why I had to get married was because of my father. I was in competition with him and didn't realize it until many years later. Every move I made as a husband and father, I compared it to what my father did or did not do with me growing up. It was a huge distraction that would cost me plenty down the road. Nevertheless, there was a wedding that needed to be planned, and Kim didn't hesitate to get started.

May 30, 2004, I was twenty-four years old, with two kids and a new wife. The wedding was awesome. I had my Aunt Annie Ruth stand in for my mother and my brother Erick as my best man. It was truly a great day seeing my son as the ring bearer being rolled down the aisle in the wagon and my beautiful little girl, in a gorgeous dress as the flower girl. The evening ended with Kazual and I taking a nap at the table.

Weeks after the wedding, I was faced with one of the biggest dilemmas in my life. One evening I was working the 2-10 shift and got an outside call from my niece. She was frantic and crying, and I could barely understand a word she was saying. After I got her to calm down, she stated that she had just been raped and she needed me to come get her. I felt my heart drop to the floor. I called my supervisor and was given permission to leave the institution. As I drove to Bellwood, I knew that I had to have my two nieces come live with me, but I did not have enough room to take in two additional children. I was already in the process of buying a home, but I would have to scrap those plans and find a bigger home.

My two nieces, were at that time staying with my dad and his wife Maggie after my sister Stacey continued to battle with substance abuse. My father and Maggie did a tremendous job taking care of my nieces and will be forever grateful for that, but I believed that the girls could use a change of scenery, especially after what just happened. I had all these plans and ideas in my head but needed to talk to Kim and see what she thought of the whole thing.

When I got to Bellwood, I could hear arguments coming from the house. I proceeded to walk in and heard my niece and Maggie having a heated exchange of inappropriate words. When I reached the basement where the two were, I heard Maggie state "you too damn fast," or something like that. Before I knew and no regard for my father's home I lost it. I said a few things that I regret and wished I could take back, but the moment had me in a state of anger and hurt. Before I knew it, Bellwood's Finest was outside the home. I explained to them what happened and I'm sure they took it easy on me because I was still in uniform. They asked me to leave, and I told them I would immediately.

When the officer left, I went right back into the house and asked my father if we could talk. Before we started, I apologized for how disrespectful I was in his home. I looked my father right in the eye and asked him to let the girls come home with me when school ends in a few weeks. We talked particulars, and then he agreed to do it. So, I grabbed a pen, a paper and wrote a note stating what we had just agreed on. I asked my father to take a ride with me, and we went to the currency exchange and had the letter notarized.

When I went back to the house, I had to speak to my niece and hear the entire story. She began explaining the story, but all I heard was "he is around the corner right now, he works in the barbershop." My eyes got wide, and my fist clenched together. I jumped in my car and drove around the block and parked right in front of the shop. I walked in and asked for the guy my niece named. The other guys in the shop all together said he was gone for the day. I stood there for a second and just looked around, totally forgetting that I was still in uniform and would probably be arrested and my employer notified if I did what I went in there to do.

I turned around and walked out feeling like I just lost all control of myself. I was storming around looking for a guy who apparently raped my niece so I could fight him, and I just had the Bellwood police ask me to leave my father's home. I needed to take a step back and cool off. As I was walking to my car, a man yelled out my name as he came behind the barbershop. I couldn't make out who the guy was until he got closer to me. When I was able to make his face out, it was the guy whom I used to work with back when I was in school, (for memory sake, let's just call him Bill). Bill, started asking why I came into the shop looking for him, did I need a cut.

After catching up a little, I explained to him why I was there. He began apologizing wholeheartedly and stated that he had no idea my niece was under aged and when he found out her age, he stopped dealing with her. He also told me that he hasn't seen my niece in months and thought this situation was over. I told him that I was just informed of this and left work to find out what was going on. I spoke to her guardian and told them my side of the story, he said. We continued to iron out the situation and asked him to continue to stay away from my niece. I apologized for coming to his job to confront him but was overloaded with anger. We shook hands and parted ways. For a second, I contemplated going back to my father's house to ask about the information I just received, but I was emotionally drained and decided to drive home to talk to Kim.

When I got home, I sat Kim down and told her about everything that happened that day. When I got to the point where I had my dad sign over his rights, she looked at me and said: "We can do it." I immediately began to cry. All the emotions I was feeling just started pouring out of me. I also cried, because I couldn't believe Kim was so open to take on two additional children without knowing how we could care for them. After I was able to gather myself, the real pressure of blending this family started to wane on me. I was scared, very scared.

After our lease was up, me, Kim and the kids moved in with her mom until I was able to secure a loan for our first home. Kim's mom was so gracious to us. She let us take her master bedroom and didn't even charge us a dime for the entire time we were there. My course of action for securing a loan was to make sure I had enough money for a down payment. I started to work sixteen hours days, three to four days a week. I was seeing less and less of my kids, and I was so caught up in the process, I forget about the people I was doing it for.

Trying to buy a house has to be one of the most nerve wrecking things there is. I started working with a mortgage company out in Oakbrook. I had a few things on my credit report that they wanted removed or paid, but other than that I was in good shape. I really didn't care where I lived, so Kim did most of the house hunting. Whenever she saw something she liked, she would set up a viewing with the realtor we hired. Looking for a home was just as draining as the purchase process. After walking into some of these homes, I nearly changed my mind and floating the idea to Kim of renting all my life. Kim and I really wanted to build our own home, but with the new recent event, we had no time for that.

Towards the end of the summer, Kim found something that she liked. It was a four bedroom single family home in the suburb of Montgomery, just northeast of Aurora. When I first saw the home, it looked just as pitiful as the others. The kitchen was painted in a rich salmon color, and the backyard was huge. Huge in the fact, that I was the only one tasked to cut and maintain it. When I went upstairs, that was when I saw what Kim saw in the home. The master bedroom was ridiculous, had a huge walk in closet and its own huge bathroom, with a Jacuzzi size tub and detached shower. The bathroom was so big I entertained putting a love seat in the corner. We both were very excited about the potential of this house. Our realtor had disclosed that the sellers wanted to sell quickly because they were finalizing a divorce. They want 224,000 for the home.

After hearing the price, the house was ugly all over again. It wasn't out of my price range but wasn't what I wanted to pay for my first house. Before I could say no, I caught a glimpse of Kim and knew she really wanted this house. Against my better judgment, I told our realtor to offer $185,000. After leaving the house, Kim was smiling from ear to ear. I was hoping the seller would take my offer, but the realtor called us immediately with the sellers counter offer of $210,000, and all closing cost paid by the sellers. My realtor told me that I should take the offer because there was another offer on the table from another buyer. In hindsight, I should have let that house go and moved on to another. Buying that house was the beginning of a lot of heartache for me. I accepted the buyer's offer and was scheduled to close in thirty days.

The day of the closing, I was quite nervous. In a few hours, I would be a homeowner, an incredible accomplishment for a young man who somehow was beating the odds. When we arrived at the title company, the sellers were already there. When I tell you, these two hated each other, it was evident. I believe this was the last thing for them to do before the divorce could be final. When I last saw the house, the front lawn was a beautiful sea of green grass, but when I went by to do a final walk through, there wasn't a green piece of lawn in sight. The entire front lawn was brown from neglect. My realtor advised me to ask the sellers for $2000.00, to have the yard treated with new sod. When the husband heard my request, he was livid. "Absolutely not," he stated, but the wife quickly intervened and stated, "no problem." That ignited another argument between the two, which lasted about a half an hour. After cooler heads prevailed, all the paperwork was signed, and I received the keys to my new home.

We all moved in a few days later, and my nieces were scheduled to come in a few weeks. As soon as we moved in, Kim was experiencing a flare up that hit her harder than usual. There was so much to do. I needed to get all three kids enrolled in school, make upgrades to the house, and take care of my wife. I was deeply feeling the pressure to get everything accomplished. The hardest thing was watching my wife suffer and unable to help her. She was going to work every day and trying to push through. The more things I got accomplished, the more things were added to the plate.

Things at work were chaotic too. One day, there was a huge fight in the day room and one of the youth, accidentally hit me in the mouth, knocking out a tooth and giving me a concussion. After leaving the emergency room, I went straight home and tried finishing some painting that needed to be done. Even the concussion couldn't keep me from trying to get all this work done. Weeks turned into months, and the pressure was insurmountable. I was moments away from completely breaking down.

One night, had to be 1am. There was a huge bang at the front door. When I jumped up to go answer it, there were at least six girls out there screaming for my niece to come outside. When they saw me open the door, they started running to a car that was waiting for them. So when they ran, I ran after them. I saw a brick in the street and picked it up and threw it towards the car. Barely missing it, I was in the middle of the street yelling, and cursing in my underwear. I went back to the house to talk to my niece about what was going on. That incident was the first of many from my niece. Things were not working out as I planned.

The straw that broke the camel's back happened one afternoon when I was at the grocery store. I got a call from Kim that changed the course of all of our lives. She called to tell me that she had reconnected with an ex-boyfriend and was confiding in him. She tried reassuring me that nothing sexual ever happened, only get togethers' and talking. At that very moment, I planned my exit from the marriage. I did not know how long it would take, but I was going to leave my wife.

For the next few months, I fell into a state of depression. The number one reason was because I thought I failed my children. I knew I had to leave their mom and the guilt was overtaking me. I was unable to work and took a leave from the job, which I believe was a month. Every day, I had trouble taking in and filtering information. I didn't eat much, and I was forgetting to pay my bills especially my mortgage. Kim and I fought and argued a lot. Friends and family tried reaching out, but I would never answer the phone. I got the energy one morning to go to the health club. When I got undressed and saw all the weight I had lost, I broke down and began to cry.

When I got the strength to return to work, I just wasn't myself. I would only work three days a week and call offed the other two days. I had become more aggressive towards the youth, challenging them to a fight and exchanging insults with them. When I went home, I slept most of the time, completely ignoring my responsibilities to my children. I didn't pray, I didn't seek help, I was just existing. I felt my heart hardening to the things I loved. I had become a shell of who I was and who I wanted to be.

CHAPTER 8

YOU RUINED IT

I had completely given up. By the time I started to feel like myself again, the damage was already done. I was six months behind on my mortgage. Not because we didn't have the money, but I had no idea I didn't pay them. One afternoon, I was cleaning out my trunk and found a box full of bills underneath the spare tire. I'm not sure how they got there, but I am sure I put them there. I thought long and hard about saving my home and saving everything else that came with it, but I was too proud to do so. I called the mortgage company and told them I had no intentions of trying to save my home. I asked for thirty days' notice of when I needed to be out. When the notice came a year and a half later, I moved my family and all the issues to another house in Oswego.

Not really sure what Kim and I said to the kids when it was time to leave. I do remember Dez, having a hard time with it. Little Kazual, was going with the flow and my oldest niece had graduated from high school and decided to move out on her own. The house we moved into was really nice and in a good school district. We got all three kids enrolled, and tried putting ourselves back together again, especially the marriage. I had hoped that the change of scenery, would do something to save a dying marriage, but after a few months, things started to escalate even further.

One evening, Kim and I got into a heated argument. Most times when we went at each other, the kids were not home, or they were asleep. But whatever the issue was this time, it could not wait until the kids were gone or asleep. What I do remember was that we were in the bedroom and we were grabbing at each other's phone. We began to push each other back and forth, and my phone fell into the toilet. There was only one thing to do after that, and that was to put her phone in the toilet next to mine. Kim curled up on the floor guarding her cell phone with her life. I was yelling and cursing and trying to pry the phone from her hands. As I jerked her back and forth, Dez, came into the room yelling asking us to stop. The look that she gave us broke my heart, and I am sure Kim's as well. She walked out of the room, and Kim and I didn't say a word. I went to the toilet to try to get my phone. I took the battery out and placed it on the counter. I went and got into the bed and pull the blanket completely over my face.

The next morning, Kim informed me that she was willing to go to counseling if I was. At first, I was not thrilled about going to see a therapist. I was and still a very private person and didn't think a therapist could help us. I called my insurance provider and got a referral from a counselor in my network. When we went to our first session, I was somewhat nervous, but hopeful there could be some breakthrough. We sat down and the hour session began. She asked all the getting to know you questions before we dove into why we were there. Kim said her piece, and I said mine. The session, in my opinion, drove us farther apart. I remember going to a few sessions and felt like it was two against one. There was no progress, no solution.

Finances was one issue along with parenting styles, trust, and forgiveness. I would call myself more diligent and a saver and Kim, a free spender. It is not necessarily the money, but the checks and balances of the money. Kim and I decided to share a checking account and have both payroll checks directly deposited there. Every pay period I tried following a system that I paid myself first and then paid bills after. Whatever money was left over after that, Kim and I could splurge a bit. Growing up like I did and dealing with money issues, I really wanted to get to a point financially, where I didn't have to think about money ever again.

So one pay period, I did an enormous amount of overtime. I told Kim the day before the deposit hit that I wanted to see how much money we had. I wanted to save at least two thousand. I told her when all the bills were paid and all checks cleared, she could go crazy. I knew that she wanted to get some things for Kazual's birthday that was coming up, I just wanted her to wait until I executed this plan. Payday came and I went to work. I got my pay stub in roll call and was geeking when I saw how well I did. When my shift was over, I went home to pay some bills and figure everything out. When I walked into the house, there was Target, and Party City bags everywhere. I looked at Kim and just lost it. I logged on to the bank site and got even more upset when I saw how much she spent.

We just had this conversation twenty-four hours ago. How could she totally disregard what we agreed on, I thought. I must admit, it seemed like an "IDGAF" moment that only made me more upset. I called Kim up to the bedroom, and I simply asked her why she did what she did. I don't remember what her answer was, but I know it didn't meet my satisfaction. I then told Kim that this share money thing was dead and I was getting my own account. With a straight face, she said if you separate the finances, we might as well separate all together. She said it with so much conviction that I knew it wasn't to be taken lightly. We went back and forward the entire night, arguing, cursing and agreeing that we should just separate.

It so happens that my father was coming to town a few days after the financial blow up I had with Kim. I needed to have the talk of all talks with my dad. I needed the one thing that escaped me thus far in my life. I needed his guidance more than ever, and I wanted to finally ask him what happened between him and my mom. I also needed to let him know how deeply it affected me. I was hoping he would give me the advice that would help me prevail in my marriage and answers to the questions that lingered with me for so long. But, what I most wanted was a deeper relationship, a stronger bond.

We decided to meet for breakfast in this tight but cozy diner in Montgomery. I got there first and tried calming all the nerves I had wrestling in my stomach. My father had no idea the interrogation he was about to endure. When he walked in, I grinned from ear to ear just like I always did. I felt like that little boy who cried when he tried taking me home. We embraced and took our seats. For the first few minutes, we exchanged pleasantries and then ordered something to eat. When the meal came, I just unleashed my first question. Dad, why did you leave mom? A small grin came upon his face like he knew he would one day have this conversation. He told me that my mother had always been a strong woman, a very strong dominating woman, which I could understand. She would always embarrass me in the company of others, and it took it toll on me, he said.

I tried dealing with it as long as I could, but after twenty plus years, enough was enough, he continued. I tried coming back a few times as you know, but every time I did, I realized it was not where I wanted to be. It was the hardest thing I had ever done, leaving her and my children. Even to this day, I regret it, he said. I thought about just enduring it all for the sake of her and you guys. He told me that my mother had been through some very tragic things growing up. Things so unbelievable that it totally broke my heart when he told me. The things he was telling me were adding up for me, which explains why my mom acted the way she did at times.

I told my father that I felt abandoned when he left. There were so many days that went by without seeing him or talking to him. I explained to him how bad it hurt when he would plan things and then not show up. The many baseball games that I had that he was absent from. When I found out Kim was pregnant and wanted him to scold me for being irresponsible, but he never did. I poured it on thick, and he saw and felt my pain. It felt like a thousand pounds of pressure being lifted off my shoulders. The conversation felt like a therapy session for the both of us. My father seemed relieved, that I asked those questions and could understand his reasoning.

Lastly, I told my father my intentions of moving out and separating from Kim. I remember him leaning back in his seat and asking the reasons why. I told him that we were simply two different people going in different directions. I told him that I didn't feel equal in the relationship any longer. There were countless explanations I gave my father, but I did not mention any of the big things. What about the kids, he asked. That's the hardest part, I explained. The very thought of leaving them brought tears to my eyes. They were so innocent and perfect, but their parents just couldn't get it together, I said. He didn't try and deter me like I wanted him too. For everything my father was, consistent was the biggest. I wanted him to tell me it was a bad idea and try harder to work it out, but the discipline I so badly wanted from him, he couldn't give.

Kim and the kids were planning to go to Georgia around the first of July and come back around the Fourth of July holiday. I planned to leave while they all were gone. I didn't tell anyone, not even Kim was aware of what I was planning. As the trip got closer, I was tying up loose ends. I switched banks and had my payroll check transferred. I found a loft style apartment in Lisle and went to check it out one day after work. The apartment was cool and was in my price range. I knew the child support money was going to hit me hard, so I had to be diligent with my expenses. I signed the lease and was scheduled to move in on July 2nd, they day after the family left for Georgia

I was so upset and petty at the time. I really wanted to make Kim feel the same amount of pain I was feeling, so I decided to take all the living room furniture with me when I move out. I wanted her to see emptiness when she returned home and opened that door. But, what I neglected to realize, was that my children would enter that door the same time she did. I found out much later how traumatic that was for them. They thought we had got robbed when they came home and Kim had to tell them what really was going on. I really wish I had handled that better, but I don't think I could have faced those little faces looking back at me. July 2nd, had come and I loaded everything I was taking at the door. I rented a U-haul truck, loaded everything and left my family.

I don't recall the conversation Kim, and I had when she returned home and found I moved out, but I do remember the shock and sadness of my kids. Weeks had gone by before I even had them over to the new apartment. When I got off work at 2pm, I would wait for them at the house until they get out of school around 3:30 and made sure I was gone before Kim got there from her job. When Kim and I did discuss the separation, we talked about financial support and a schedule for the kids. I began searching for additional furniture so it would be somewhat comfortable when they came by. My apartment was the size of the living room where the kids lived, and I knew that would be a shock for them.

I was so nervous when I had them for the weekend that first time. Having all of us crammed up in the little space was tough and I know the kids didn't like being there. I tried staying out of the apartment as much as possible. We went to the movies, out to eat, and the park. It was a struggle financially and emotionally trying to make them as comfortable as possible. Many times I thought of breaking the lease and going back to my wife and kids, but other aspects of my life were beginning to thrive. I felt free, for the first time in years. Not free from my children or responsibility, but free to think clearly. I started working on things that were important to my own happiness, and it felt amazing.

Three months after I moved out, I decided to take a promotion at work. My new title was Juvenile Justice Supervisor, and I was only Twenty-Nine. It was a great accomplishment for me, and I took my new responsibilities seriously. I woke up one morning and decided to buy the car of my dreams. I searched the Internet and found a good price on a 2004 Range Rover. Everything seemed to be looking up for me, but I missed my children desperately and often cried many nights wondering if I was ruining their lives. Whenever I had the kids, I would ask them if they wanted to talk about was what going on and if they were ok. They would always tell me that they were fine, but I always sensed something different especially from Dez.

Unable to control the emotional phases in my life, I decided to seek professional help, but this time, instead of a licensed therapist, I confided in a man I had known for many years prior and always treated me like a son. Edward Johnson, was my supervisor when I started with the Illinois Department of Corrections/Juvenile Justice. He had a strong presence about himself and had the respect of everyone he encountered. One year, a group of us wanted to start a bible study group and asked Mr. Johnson, if we could have it at his house and if he would lead the group. Mr. Johnson was also an ordained minister, and you could see God's Glory all over him.

I enjoyed the Monday night bible study groups because after we discussed the topic of the day, we would take time to just talk as men. He was and still had a way of explaining things that made me want to be better than I was. We had gotten so close that, I started calling him pops and he referred and treated me like a son. Whenever I needed advice or just some guidance, he was always there for me. When I would mess up at work, he was fair and just. Sitting me down and explaining that I had to learn to carry myself better than I was. If it had not been for his leadership, I would not have been able to secure that promotion. His love and kindness will forever be appreciated.

So when I went to see Mr. Johnson about the issues I was facing, I was extremely nervous. I knew that me separating from Kim, would not be approved by him. I walked into the living room and was ready to lay it all on him. I believe I spoke for thirty straight minutes before he said a word. He just listened and nodded. When I was done talking, he asked me what it was I wanted, and I told him, I just want to be free. Free from responsibility, he asked. No, I answered. Freedom of the mind. I want my mind and thoughts to finally be free. No more arguing, no more fights. I am not the man for Kim, and I have to stop pretending that I am, I explained.

And the kids, he asked. There are many days that I have been home with the kids, but my mind and spirit was elsewhere, I said. In the simplest form, Mr. Johnson said I know how much you love your kids, and Kim too. If you don't find happiness within yourself, you can't give happiness to no one else. Go out and find your truth. Ask God for guidance and strength, he said. I tried my hardest to live by his advice.

For the next few months, I struggled with the separation from the kids. What was bothering me the most, was the one thing I yearned for as a kid, and that was to have my father around. The only difference between my father and I was that I was invested in their feelings and recovery. Things came full circle for me, when one day, I took the kids out to dinner. We laughed and talked like never before. My babies were doing well in school and seemed to have adjusted to two different households. When it was time to drop them off, I pulled into the driveway, they unhooked the seat belts and hopped out of the car. As they were walking up to the door, they both turned around and waved goodbye. I erupted in tears and yelled uncontrollably.

For the next few minutes, I was unable to move. I tried numerous times to gather myself, but every time I thought I was good, it started again.

I picked up my phone and tried calling Mr. Johnson, but it went to voicemail. I decided to turn the radio on to drown out my own sobbing, and it worked. I drove home and immediately got into the bed. I started experiencing things that I never felt before. My heart started racing, so fast that I was sure I was having a heart attack. My leg began to twitch, and I was unable to stop it. For some reason, I had energy like I drank ten Red Bulls, but also was dead tired. I was experiencing my first bout with Anxiety, which has stayed with me even to this day.

CHAPTER NINE

COMMON GROUND

Kim and I Divorced, in November 2014, but before that, years had gone by and the kids were coming into their own as individuals and both Kim and I were looking forward to starting new lives with new people. In 2015, Kim married a wonderful guy named Charles, which the kids have grown to love a lot. When Kim told me about the nuptials, I asked her if it was ok to call and introduce myself to him. She agreed and texted me his number. We talked for a while about fatherhood and respecting each other's space within this new blended family. I mentioned to Charles that Kim and I hate each other six months out of the year, so just disregard our battles. We laughed about it, and he said he understood.

A year later, I married the true love of my life Tennille Townes. In all my years, I have never met a woman who wanted to bring out the best in me and thats exactly what she did. She challenged me to be better than I ever imagined I could be and I knew her love was genuine and without conditions. We had known each other in high school, but never talked or crossed each other's path. It was because of Facebook that we talked so many years later. We decided to go on a date, and when I saw her in person, I immediately knew that one day, I would be her husband. During dinner, we caught up on all the things going on in our lives, especially the complicated situation I was in with Kim. Over the next couple of months, we struggled to identify what type of relationship we were in. She expressed many times that she cared for me but I had to make my divorce final, and I agreed.

When I spoke to her about opening my own Personal Training Business, she helped me figure out my business name, logo, and Marketing ideas. She was so supportive and determined to see this venture succeed for me. I had never previously, had so much love and support coming from one individual. I married my love on Christmas Eve, 2016 in a beautiful ceremony on the deck atop the Willis Tower. Even to this day, she is the greatest friend I have ever had.

Tennille was a package deal, and when we got married, I became a stepfather to Madison and Morgan. These two bundles are identical twins that have a yearning to learn any and everything. Their goal is to one day graduate from Harvard and Yale. Although I have never met their father, I have a huge respect for who he is to them. We talk on occasion and the mutual respect is evident. We have the same goal, just like with Kim's Husband, and that is to raise productive children. Three fathers, mixed in trying to figure things out on the fly. I know it isn't easy for any one of us.

One of the things I wanted to do and spoke to Kim about occasionally was Kazual coming to live with me when he started his sophomore year. For years previously, I would ask Kazual, if that was something he wanted to do and he would always say yes. I would just remind him that there were so many things I needed to teach him as he got closer to graduation and went off to college. It wasn't anything that Kim was doing wrong, I just wanted to have some time to help him in what could be the most crucial time in his life. I thought about when I was his age and needed my father to help me through those tough years.

So, one day out of the blue and a year earlier than I anticipated, Kazual came to me and said he thought it was time he came live with me. I asked him if there was something wrong in the house and he said, "No." I asked if he and Charles were getting along ok, and he said ''yes." Dad, I just think that with Dez about to graduate and heading off to college, this would be the perfect time for us to do this, he said. I took a deep breath and explained to him that I'm 100 percent sure your mother is going to freak out about this. Are you sure you are ready to talk to her about this, and he said "yes."

I called Kim and asked if she can have dinner with Kazual and I and she agreed. I did not tell her what the meeting was about, but I'm sure she had an idea. Every day, I would call my son and ask him the same question; are you sure you are ready to talk to your mom, and every time, he answered "yes." The day of the meeting, I was nervous as hell. I knew Kim would object to the idea, but was hoping since Kazual was in favor of it, she would consider it.

When we all got to the restaurant, I waited till after the meal was over to bring up the idea. I was hungry and was really looking forward to the salmon I ordered. When Dinner was over, I came out with it, and Kazual cosigned the whole thing. She was nice enough to let us complete our speech, and when we were done, she quietly said: "Absolutely not." I wasn't too upset, I knew this would be her reaction, but I think Kazual was taken aback by it. We all finished our drinks and parted ways in good spirits. I told Kazual I would call him tomorrow, to talk about what happened.

A few months went by, and we both were still adamant that it was time for Kazual to come stay with me. I pondered it for a few days and talked to my wife about it, and decided I was going to talk to Kim again, this time with everyone involved, except my wife, she was at work. When I got to the house, everyone gathered around the kitchen, and I asked Kim again if Kazual could come stay with me. This time Kim reaction was not as polite as the last time. She started yelling and cursing me out. She blamed me for putting this idea in Kazual's head. I started to yell back completely disrespecting Charles's home. The more she yelled, the more I yelled.

When I tried calming down, I kept asking Kim to just talk to Kazual and try to understand why he wants to stay with me. I went on to say that it was not a knock on you and that you are a wonderful mother. She wasn't hearing any of that, and called me a bitch and wanted to put her hands on me. I politely told her that if she did, we all would be fighting in here today, so she might want to call the police before she hits me. Kim and I had completely lost our way and let emotions make us look like fools in front of our children. There was no reason for us to disrespect each other like that, but there is a lot of hurts there.

I left, but before I did I apologized to Charles for my behavior in his home.

I left that house heated. I tried calling Tennille, but I couldn't talk, I was that pissed. When I was able to gather myself, it dawned on me that my kids just saw the worst in me and their mom. I wanted to call them but had no words to express my shame and regrets. I wondered if I put Kazual in a bad predicament. He didn't want to disappoint his mom, but he felt like he did. It was my obligation to nurture any decision my children wanted to explore. My anger turned into validation that I was a good father, no matter how often I felt like I let my children down. Even though their mother and I didn't work out, I never left them, never!

So that morning, I decided to keep fighting for what my son had asked me for. I called a lawyer and made an appointment to talk about the issue I was having. I still hadn't spoken to Kazual or Dez. I truly didn't know what to say. I just thought I would give it some more time. When I sat down with the lawyer, I explained to her everything that happened thus far, and she thought I had a great chance of winning custody. She explained the law to me and said the only thing your son needs to do is tell the judge where he wants to be. For a minute, I got truly excited, and then it dawned on me that I would be putting my son in a very awkward position. I didn't want him to have to publicly choose me or his mom. I knew how much he didn't want to disappoint her, and I could not put him into that situation. A few days later, I called Kazual and told him that he should stay with his mom for the foreseeable future and maybe one day, she might have a change of heart. It broke my heart to tell him that.

Kim and I were definitely on bad terms after the custody situation and pretty much have not seen each other in months. I knew that was going to change soon because Dez was about to graduate from high school. I was really nervous about the graduation, for the last few months I was feeling like the odd man out. Before Kim got married, I was able to stop by the house pretty much every day to check on the kids. Now, with my kids getting older and having and wanting to spend less time with me, I definitely felt some kind of way. It was a large adjustment that I didn't have a grip on.

The morning of the graduation, I was as ready as I was ever going to be. The ceremony was in Dekalb, Illinois, about forty minutes from my home. The forty minutes was definitely needed. It gave me time to compose myself and relinquish these feelings that I was harboring. When I reached the convention center, I spotted Kim, Kazual, and Charles. They looked like the ideal family, going to celebrate the achievement of another child. For a second, I did wish I was in that situation. I still to this day worry that the decisions I made so long ago wouldn't have a negative impact on Dez and Kazual. And even though they are showered with love, sometimes it hits home just like with my father.

The ceremony was beautiful, and when Dez name was called, we all shouted and yelled. When the ceremony was over, I hugged and congratulated my daughter.

She asked if I would be joining them for dinner and I said I couldn't. The truth was, I still felt like I was there by accident. I gave her one final hug and kiss, and I headed home. The entire ride home I felt like crap. I knew I had done an outstanding job as a father. I started reflecting on how I got to this very point. I thought about the day Dez was born and the struggles I had buying just to buy diapers. I remember taking her to school on that first day of Kindergarten. Everything that I thought I was missing from my father, I gave to my children a hundred times over. The pressure of not doing enough, not being enough had to come to an end. Driving down that expressway, I learned how to accept my past and all the good that came from those heartaches. I'm finally free from the prison of my own mind. I can move forward, and be "My Father's Son."

MEET THE AUTHOR

Darrick Campbell, is an adviser, author, and Speaker. He is compelled to write about things that helps you to see things a little different than you may see them initially. There were times when life seemed to have gotten the best of him, and writing is the tool he used to rebuild myself. He speaks mainly from the "black male" perspective, fatherhood, faith, and health. Those writings are opinions that Darrick believe will create great thought provoking discussions. Darrick is a husband, father and friend! He loves his wife, his kids don't text back and God is Dope!

CONTACT DARRICK

focusgroup1980@gmail.com